Saintélangues

Niv.0

Bernard Garde

Copyright © 2016 by Bernard GARDE
All rights reserved – Tous droits réservés
Dépôt légal deuxième trimestre 2016
ISBN 978-2-913283-62-6   -   EAN 9782913283626
Conception, impression & distribution via Createspace et Amazon

A toutes les victimes des excès de l'enseignement-spectacle au détriment de l'apprentissage autonome et bilingue.

PREAMBULE

La méthode autonome d'apprentissage accéléré dont la première étape vous est proposée ici est le fruit de plus de trente années d'expérience et de découvertes pratiques sur l'auto-apprentissage bilingue, dont les résultats sans précédents vous sont décrits et commentés dans le Rapport Saintélangues, également disponible sur Amazon.fr.

Ce premier volume est réservé à tout débutant ou « re-débutant intégral » en anglais, désireux de s'approprier activement les cinq premiers paliers de compétences d'expression et de construction sans lesquels il est rigoureusement impossible de parler correctement, au sens le plus basique et usuel du terme.

L'objectif de ce « niveau 0 » accéléré est de franchir ces toutes premières étapes structurales de façon motivante grâce à la progressivité et la densité des phrases à construire, avec le plaisir de s'évaluer à chaque page et la garantie de transformer très facilement la réflexion en réflexe.

Idéalement prévus pour une pratique individuelle, ces exercices peuvent également se concevoir en binôme ou « pair work », voire en groupe *a fortiori*, et même de façon directement orale en cas de révision. Mais la forme écrite recommandée dans le mode d'emploi qui suit est indispensable pour garantir à la fois une installation grammaticale définitive et une mémorisation sans effort du vocabulaire proposé.

MODE D'EMPLOI

Lire attentivement le résumé grammatical de la première étape en **observant les différences signalées entre le français et l'anglais**. Il est pratique d'utiliser des « post-it » afin de retrouver plus facilement les pages de vocabulaire et de grammaire pendant la réalisation d'un exercice.

Sans rien apprendre par cœur, et **en prenant soin de cacher la page de droite qui servira de corrigé**, utiliser aussi souvent que nécessaire le vocabulaire et le résumé grammatical de l'étape en cours d'étude pour « traduire », ou plus précisément « construire », les 20 phrases du premier exercice en écrivant sur un cahier ou une feuille annexe.

Une fois la première page terminée, comparer attentivement sa production avec le corrigé de la page de droite, et rectifier au besoin (en rouge de préférence) en analysant le pourquoi de son erreur, le cas échéant.

Il suffit de procéder de la même façon pour l'exercice suivant, sans jamais avoir besoin de refaire la même page, et vous aurez le plaisir de voir rapidement diminuer, puis disparaître, les corrections nécessaires. (L'important étant de ne jamais s'attaquer à un nouvel exercice sans avoir d'abord corrigé soigneusement le précédent, *of course !*)

REMARQUES IMPORTANTES

Ce Niveau 0 de Saintélangues est spécialement conçu pour accélérer la mise en place des structures de base les plus indispensables en toute situation. Le vocabulaire proposé dans ce volume est donc volontairement très limité comparé aux lexiques des 9 ouvrages suivants des niveaux 0, 1 et 2 de la même méthode.

Le but est de permettre aux **re-débutants** d'accéder directement au Niveau 1 après cette compilation accélérée du Niveau 0. Il n'y a par ailleurs aucun risque ultérieur en matière de vocabulaire puisque celui du Niveau 0 se trouve entièrement inclus dans le Niveau 1. Cela dit, **un débutant intégral** aura toujours intérêt à accomplir le parcours 0A/0B/0C avant le niveau 1, et ce Niv.0 lui aura permis d'étaler le tout premier module de 0A en trois étapes encore plus progressives.

Le vocabulaire disponible en fin d'ouvrage est « phonétisé à la française » afin de faciliter la prononciation du débutant intégral, et un enregistrement complet est également disponible sur Amazon.fr pour améliorer compréhension et prononciation par écoute, dictée et répétition.

Now enjoy yourself with Saintélangues !

B.G.

Résumé Grammatical Etape 0/1

Le présent simple :

Le présent simple se "conjugue" en utilisant l'infinitif sans "to" et en ajoutant seulement un "s" pour la troisième personne du singulier (il, elle) :

travailler = to work (infinitif) se conjugue ainsi au présent :
I work, you work, he/she/it **works**, we work, you work, they work.
(he = il (M), she = elle (F), it = il ou elle en parlant d'un objet ou animal)

La forme affirmative :

En anglais, la forme affirmative **Sujet + Verbe + Complément** est toujours la même quel que soit le complément (nom, ou pronom) :

Je connais **Jim** = I know **Jim**
Je **le** connais = I know **him** (Je connais lui)
En anglais, le pronom complément est donc toujours placé **après** le verbe.

L'adjectif (épithète) :

En anglais, l'adjectif est toujours invariable (ni pluriel, ni féminin, ni masculin) et systématiquement placé devant le nom qu'il qualifie :

Une grosse voiture = A big car.
Deux nouvelles voitures américaines = Two new American cars.
(Noter que les adjectifs de nationalité s'écrivent avec une majuscule).

Conjuguaisons des verbes (et auxiliaires) être et avoir au présent :

Etre = **to be** : I **am**, you **are**, he/she/it **is**, we **are**, you **are**, they **are**.
(abbrev.: I'm, you're, he's, she's, it's, we're, you're, they're.)

Avoir = **to have** : I have, you have, he/she/it **has**, we have, you have, they have.
(Abbrev.: I've got, you've got, he/she/it's got, we've got, you've got, they've got)

En utilisant ces éléments de grammaire ainsi que le vocabulaire en fin d'ouvrage, traduire, puis corriger chaque page des exercices qui suivent.

1 - Elle me connaît.

2 - Nous les aimons.

3 - Il nous rencontre ici.

4 - Je vis avec elle.

5 - Ils vous aiment.

6 - Nous les connaissons.

7 - Ils sont avec nous.

8 - Je travaille avec eux.

9 - Je sais qu'ils sont ici.

10 - Il veut te rencontrer.

11 - Il préfère être avec moi.

12 - Je les connais.

13 - Vous travaillez avec lui.

14 - Elles nous aiment.

15 - Elle est avec lui.

16 - Ils vivent avec moi.

17 - Je la rencontre ici.

18 - Ils sont avec toi.

19 - Ils nous connaissent.

20 - Elle travaille avec moi.

1 - She knows me.

2 - We like/love them.

3 - He meets us here.

4 - I live with her.

5 - They like/love you.

6 - We know them.

7 - They are with us.

8 - I work with them.

9 - I know they are here.

10 - He wants to meet you.

11 - He prefers to be with me.

12 - I know them.

13 - You work with him.

14 - They like/love us.

15 - She is with him.

16 - They live with me.

17 - I meet her here.

18 - They are with you.

19 - They know us.

20 - She works with me.

1 - Ils savent que je suis ici.

2 - Elles vivent avec nous.

3 - Je sais qu'ils sont ici.

4 - Vous les aimez.

5 - Elle travaille avec toi.

6 - Tu les rencontres ici.

7 - Nous savons qu'elle t'aime.

8 - Je suis avec eux.

9 - Ils te connaissent.

10 - Nous sommes avec elles.

11 - Tu veux les rencontrer.

12 - Elles me connaissent.

13 - Il travaille avec moi.

14 - Nous sommes avec eux.

15 - Vous vivez avec lui.

16 - Ils préfèrent me rencontrer.

17 - J'aime travailler avec elle.

18 - Ils sont ici avec moi.

19 - Ils veulent la rencontrer.

20 - Vous les connaissez.

1 - They know I'm here.

2 - They live with us.

3 - I know they are here.

4 - You like/love them.

5 - She works with you.

6 - You meet them here.

7 - We know she loves/likes you.

8 - I am with them.

9 - They know you.

10 - We are with them.

11 - You want to meet them.

12 - They know me.

13 - He works with me.

14 - We are with them.

15 - You live with him.

16 - They prefer to meet me.

17 - I like to work with her.

18 - They are here with me.

19 - They want to meet her.

20 - You know them.

1 - J'aime cette voiture.

2 - Ils te connaissent.

3 - Tu préfères cette maison.

4 - Elle travaille avec moi.

5 - Ils sont ici avec moi.

6 - Il travaille à Glasgow.

7 - Nous les connaissons.

8 - Tu as une nouvelle adresse.

9 - Ils sont avec elle.

10 - J'ai trois soeurs.

11 - Nous sommes amis.

12 - Elle préfère vivre ici.

13 - Nous connaissons ces enfants.

14 - Ils aiment cette vieille maison.

15 - Elle veut me rencontrer.

16 - Nous préférons travailler ici.

17 - Ils sont avec nous à Paris.

18 - Je veux le rencontrer ici.

19 - Cette voiture est pour nous.

20 - Je connais ce garçon.

1 - I like this/that car.

2 - They know you.

3 - You prefer this/that house.

4 - She works with me.

5 - They are here with me.

6 - He works in Glasgow.

7 - We know them.

8 - You have (You've got) a new address.

9 - They are with her.

10 - I have (I've got) three sisters.

11 - We are friends.

12 - She prefers to live here.

13 - We know these children.

14 - They like this/that old house.

15 - She wants to meet me.

16 - We prefer to work here.

17 - They are with us in Paris.

18 - I want to meet him here.

19 - This/That car is for us.

20 - I know this/that boy.

1 - Cette fille travaille avec toi.

2 - Nous sommes à Cork avec lui.

3 - Il préfère me rencontrer ici.

4 - Elles sont dans cette voiture.

5 - Je préfère ce nouveau restaurant.

6 - Elle veut le rencontrer ici.

7 - Ils savent que je suis avec toi.

8 - Ils nous rencontrent à Paris.

9 - Nous travaillons avec eux.

10 - Il préfère venir avec elle.

11 - Ils ont un nouveau garage.

12 - Elle a un cousin en France.

13 - Nous sommes ici avec eux.

14 – Il veut te rencontrer ici.

15 - Ils ont trois enfants.

16 - Je sais qu'elle est avec toi.

17 - Ils veulent te rencontrer à Leeds.

18 - Nous préférons travailler avec vous.

19 - Les enfants sont avec elle.

20 - Il veut avoir une nouvelle voiture.

1 - This/That girl works with you.

2 - We are in Cork with him.

3 - He prefers to meet me here.

4 - They are in this/that car.

5 - I prefer this/that new restaurant.

6 - She wants to meet him here.

7 - They know I am with you.

8 - They meet us in Paris.

9 - We work with them.

10 - He prefers to come with her.

11 - They have (They've got) a new garage.

12 - She has (She's got) a cousin in France.

13 - We are here with them.

14 – He wants to meet you here.

15 - They have (They've got) three children.

16 - I know she is with you.

17 - They want to meet you in Leeds.

18 - We prefer to work with you.

19 - The children are with her.

20 - He wants to have a new car.

1 - Les Wilson sont dans cette voiture.

2 - Nous savons qu'elles sont amies.

3 - Cette jeune fille est une cousine.

4 - Nous voulons les rencontrer.

5 - Il sait que je suis ici avec toi.

6 - Elle a un nouvel appartement.

7 - Ils travaillent avec elle à Oxford.

8 - Nous connaissons ces filles.

9 - Elle préfère être ici avec nous.

10 - Ils ont trois amis à Londres.

11 - Cette nouvelle voiture est pour moi.

12 - Elle sait que je te connais.

13 - Je préfère les rencontrer ici.

14 - Elle aime ce vieux restaurant.

15 - Nous travaillons avec elle.

16 - Elle préfère venir avec lui.

17 - Ils veulent nous rencontrer.

18 - Vous connaissez cet homme.

19 - Ils savent qu'elle m'aime.

20 - Je vis avec elle à Birmingham.

1 - The Wilsons are in this/that car.

2 - We know they are friends.

3 - This/That young girl is a cousin.

4 - We want to meet them.

5 - He knows I am (I'm) here with you.

6 - She has (She's got) a new flat.

7 - They work with her in Oxford.

8 - We know these girls.

9 - She prefers to be here with us.

10 - They have (They've got) three friends in London.

11 - This/That new car is for me.

12 - She knows I know you.

13 - I prefer to meet them here.

14 - She likes this/that old restaurant.

15 - We work with her.

16 - She prefers to come with him.

17 - They want to meet us.

18 - You know this/that man.

19 - They know she loves/likes me.

20 - I live with her in Birmingham.

1- Nous savons qu'elles sont ici.
2 - J'aime travailler avec eux.
3 - Ces enfants vous connaissent.
4 - Ils ont une nouvelle adresse.
5 - Je connais ces femmes.
6 - Cet homme veut travailler avec toi.
7 - Elle préfère habiter ici avec moi.
8 - Nous avons quatre enfants.
9 - Elle veut avoir une nouvelle voiture.
10 - Ils ont un appartement à Cambridge.
11 - Ces garçons sont avec nous.
12 - Nous voulons la rencontrer avec toi.
13 - Elle sait que je suis ici avec lui.
14 - Ils préfèrent venir avec elle.
15 - Ces filles sont avec ma nièce.
16 - Je sais qu'elle t'aime.
17 - Ils travaillent ici avec moi.
18 - Nous sommes ici avec eux.
19 - Tu sais qu'ils sont amis.
20 – Elle veut travailler avec lui.

1- We know they are here.

2 - I like to work with them.

3 - These children know you.

4 - They have (They've got) a new address.

5 - I know these women.

6 - This/That man wants to work with you.

7 - She prefers to live here with me.

8 - We have (We've got) four children.

9 - She wants to have a new car.

10 - They have (They've got) a flat in Cambridge.

11 - These boys are with us.

12 - We want to meet her with you.

13 - She knows I am here with him.

14 - They prefer to come with her.

15 - These girls are with my niece.

16 - I know she loves/likes you.

17 - They work here with me.

18 - We are (We're) here with them.

19 - You know they are friends.

20 - She wants to work with him.

1 - Nous préférons venir avec eux.

2 - Ils sont avec toi à Liverpool.

3 - Elle a un nouvel ami à Watford.

4 - Je sais qu'il a une voiture.

5 - Ils connaissent ce vieil appartement.

6 - Ils sont avec lui dans cette voiture.

7 - Elle sait que j'ai un nouvel ami.

8 - Je préfère la rencontrer ici.

9 - Il sait que je travaille avec elle.

10 - Nous avons une nouvelle adresse.

11 - Je sais que ces enfants sont français.

12 - Il veut me rencontrer ici avec toi.

13 - Il sait que Betty est avec moi.

14 - Je veux travailler avec eux.

15 - Ils préfèrent vivre avec toi.

16 - Nous savons qu'elle les aime.

17 - Ils ont une maison en Angleterre.

18 - Il sait que nous sommes avec toi.

19 - Cette nouvelle maison est pour nous.

20 - Nous sommes avec elle dans la voiture.

1 - We prefer to come with them.

2 - They are with you in Liverpool.

3 - She has (She's got) a new friend in Watford.

4 - I know he has (he's got) a car.

5 - They know this/that old flat.

6 - They are with him in this/that car.

7 - She knows I have (I've got) a new friend.

8 - I prefer to meet her here.

9 - He knows I work with her.

10 - We have (We've got) a new address.

11 - I know these children are French.

12 - He wants to meet me here with you.

13 - He knows Betty is with me.

14 - I want to work with them.

15 - They prefer to live with you.

16 - We know she loves/likes them.

17 - They have (They've got) a house in England.

18 - He knows we are with you.

19 - This/That new house is for us.

20 - We are (We're) with her in the car.

1 - Elle est avec lui dans la cuisine.

2 - Je veux travailler avec lui à Paris.

3 - Il me connaît parce que j'habite ici.

4 - Nous savons qu'elle vous aime.

5 - Ils nous rencontrent ici avec elle.

6 - Elle préfère travailler avec moi.

7 - J'ai un nouvel ami à Manchester.

8 - Ils ont cette vieille voiture.

9 - Nous sommes à Madrid avec eux.

10 - Ils savent que tu travailles avec moi.

11 - Je préfère être ici avec eux.

12 - Ils veulent le rencontrer ici.

13 - Nous savons qu'ils sont avec elle.

14 - Cette femme nous connaît.

15 - J'ai une nouvelle adresse à Cork.

16 - Vous voulez travailler avec eux.

17 - Je sais qu'il travaille avec toi.

18 - Elles sont avec lui dans cette voiture.

19 - Elle sait que nous sommes amis.

20 - Nous avons deux cousins à Leeds.

1 - She is with him in the kitchen.

2 - I want to work with him in Paris.

3 - He knows me because I live here.

4 - We know she loves/likes you.

5 - They meet us here with her.

6 - She prefers to work with me.

7 - I have (I've got) a new friend in Manchester.

8 - They have (They've got) this/that old car.

9 - We are in Madrid with them.

10 - They know you work with me.

11 - I prefer to be here with them.

12 - They want to meet him here.

13 - We know they are with her.

14 - This/That woman knows us.

15 - I have (I've got) a new address in Cork.

16 - You want to work with them.

17 - I know he works with you.

18 - They are (They're) with him in this/that car.

19 - She knows we are friends.

20 - We have (We've got) two cousins in Leeds.

1 - Ces jeunes garçons sont anglais.

2 - Elle a une nouvelle voiture française.

3 - Nous savons qu'ils aiment travailler.

4 - Il préfère venir avec elle.

5 - Ils connaissent cette vieille maison.

6 - Nous sommes ici avec elle.

7 - Je sais qu'ils ont trois voitures.

8 - Ils veulent nous rencontrer ici.

9 - Elles savent que je suis ici avec toi.

10 - Je préfère les rencontrer à Watford.

11 - Il me connaît parce que je travaille ici.

12 - Je sais qu'il vit avec toi à Liverpool.

13 - Elle veut me rencontrer dans ce restaurant.

14 - Je suis ici parce que tu veux me rencontrer.

15 - Nous avons un nouvel appartement.

16 - Elle sait que tu es ici avec moi.

17 - Je sais que vous aimez ces enfants.

18 - Ils veulent me rencontrer à Londres.

19 - Elle préfère venir avec eux.

20 - Nous avons leur nouvelle adresse.

1 - These young boys are English.

2 - She has (She's got) a new French car.

3 - We know they like to work.

4 - He prefers to come with her.

5 - They know this/that old house.

6 - We are (We're) here with her.

7 - I know they have (They've got) three cars.

8 - They want to meet us here.

9 - They know I am (I'm) here with you.

10 - I prefer to meet them in Watford.

11 - He knows me because I work here.

12 - I know he lives with you in Liverpool.

13 - She wants to meet me in this/that restaurant.

14 - I am (I'm) here because you want to meet me.

15 - We have (We've got) a new flat.

16 - She knows you are (you're) here with me.

17 - I know you love/like these children.

18 - They want to meet me in London.

19 - She prefers to come with them.

20 - We have (We've got) their new address.

1 - Ces hommes travaillent avec nous.

2 - Je sais que cette femme est anglaise.

3 - Elle veut te rencontrer avec moi.

4 - Ces filles préfèrent être avec toi.

5 - Elle sait que je travaille ici avec lui.

6 - Nous avons trois amis à Bath.

7 - Il veut nous rencontrer dans ce restaurant.

8 - Vous savez que je les aime.

9 - Cette vieille voiture est pour nous.

10 - Nous sommes avec elles à Paris.

11 - Ils savent que nous sommes amis.

12 - Cette nouvelle maison est pour eux.

13 - Elle a un vieil oncle à Leeds.

14 - Ces enfants préfèrent être avec moi.

15 - Cet enfant sait que je suis avec toi.

16 - Je veux travailler ici avec eux.

17 - Ils préfèrent te rencontrer avec elle.

18 - Elle travaille ici avec vous.

19 - Nous avons une nièce à Boston.

20 - Il connaît mon nom parce que je travaille ici.

1 - These men work with us.

2 - I know this/that woman is English.

3 - She wants to meet you with me.

4 - These girls prefer to be with you.

5 - She knows I work here with him.

6 - We have (We've got) three friends in Bath.

7 - He wants to meet us in this/that restaurant.

8 - You know I love/like them.

9 - This/That old car is for us.

10 - We are (We're) with them in Paris.

11 - They know we are friends.

12 - This/That new house is for them.

13 - She has (She's got) an old uncle in Leeds.

14 - These children prefer to be with me.

15 - This child knows I am (I'm) with you.

16 - I want to work here with them.

17 - They prefer to meet you with her.

18 - She works here with you.

19 - We have (We've got) a niece in Boston.

20 - He knows my name because I work here.

1 - Il sait que nous sommes avec eux.

2 - Je les rencontre à Liverpool.

3 - Nous avons une nouvelle voiture française.

4 - Elle connaît ce nouveau restaurant.

5 - Ils préfèrent habiter à Londres.

6 - Je sais qu'il est ici avec les Spencer.

7 - Les enfants sont dans le jardin.

8 - Elle veut travailler ici avec moi.

9 - Ce garçon connaît une nouvelle adresse.

10 - Nous préférons les rencontrer à Hull.

11 - Elle sait que cet homme travaille avec moi.

12 - Il veut avoir un nouvel appartement.

13 - Les parents sont avec lui dans le garage.

14 - J'ai un nouvel ami en Amérique.

15 - Ces gens savent que nous sommes ici.

16 - Ils aiment vivre dans cette maison.

17 - Elle préfère nous rencontrer à Leeds.

18 - Les enfants sont dans la salle de bain.

19 - Je sais que les Parker aiment ce restaurant.

20 - Cette jeune femme veut te rencontrer.

1 - He knows we are with them.

2 - I meet them in Liverpool.

3 - We have (We've got) a new French car.

4 - She knows this/that new restaurant.

5 - They prefer to live in London.

6 - I know he is (he's) here with the Spencers.

7 - The children are in the garden.

8 - She wants to work here with me.

9 - This/That boy knows a new address.

10 - We prefer to meet them in Hull.

11 - She knows this/that man works with me.

12 - He wants to have a new flat.

13 - The parents are with him in the garage.

14 - I have (I've got) a new friend in America.

15 - These people know we are here.

16 - They like to live in this house.

17 - She prefers to meet us in Leeds.

18 - The children are in the bathroom.

19 - I know the Parkers like this/that restaurant.

20 - This/That young woman wants to meet you.

1 - Il travaille avec eux dans ce restaurant.
2 - Ces gens veulent habiter à Birmingham.
3 - Je sais qu'elle préfère venir avec lui.
4 - Ils sont avec nous dans le garage.
5 - Nous préférons travailler ici avec elle.
6 - Ce jeune homme veut travailler avec toi.
7 - Ils préfèrent aller à Londres avec lui.
8 - Cette vieille maison est pour M. Smith.
9 - Il sait que je travaille ici avec Linda.
10- Ils ont une nouvelle voiture anglaise.
11 – Je sais que cette fille travaille avec eux.
12 - Je la rencontre ici avec ce jeune homme.
13 - Nous préférons travailler dans le salon.
14 - Tu sais qu'ils sont avec elle à Watford.
15 - Elle a deux fils et trois filles.
16 - Ces gens savent que je veux les rencontrer.
17 - Elle sait que j'aime ce nouveau jardin.
18 - Je préfère travailler dans la cuisine.
19 - Elle sait que nous avons trois chambres.
20 - Ces jeunes gens veulent travailler avec moi.

1 - He works with them in this/that restaurant.

2 - These people want to live in Birmingham.

3 - I know she prefers to come with him.

4 - They are with us in the garage.

5 - We prefer to work here with her.

6 - This/That young man wants to work with you.

7 - They prefer to go to London with him.

8 - This/That old house is for Mr. Smith.

9 - He knows I work here with Linda.

10- They have (They've got) a new English car.

11 – I know this/that girl works with them.

12 - I meet her here with this/that young man.

13 - We prefer to work in the living-room.

14 - You know they are with her in Watford.

15 - She has (She's got) two sons and three daughters.

16 - These people know I want to meet them.

17 - She knows I like this/that new garden.

18 - I prefer to work in the kitchen.

19 - She knows we have (got) three bedrooms.

20 - These young people want to work with me.

Résumé Grammatical Etape 0/2

L'adjectif possessif

En anglais, l'adjectif possessif ne dépend pas de la chose ou personne possédée :

Ma voiture, **mon** livre, **mes** amis = **My** car, **my** book, **my** friends.

Par contre pour la troisième personne du singulier, l'adjectif possessif anglais varie selon le « possesseur » masculin, féminin ou neutre (objet) :

Son livre (à **lui**) = **his** book
Son livre (à **elle**) = **her** book
Son prix (en parlant d'un **objet**) = **its** price.

Petit truc mnémotechnique pour ne pas mélanger masculin et féminin :

dans « his » il y a un « i » comme pour « lui »
dans « her » il y a un « e » comme pour « elle »

La liste çi-dessous est rappelée en fin de vocabulaire :

mon, ma, mes	my
ton, ta, tes	your
son, sa, ses	**his** (à lui), **her** (à elle), **its** (objet)
notre, nos	our
votre, vos	your
leur(s) (+nom)	their

Attention, ne pas confondre "leur" complément et "leur" possessif.

Je leur téléphone = I phone **them**.　　(leur + verbe = them)
Je connais leur fils = I know **their** son.　(leur + nom = their)

En utilisant ces éléments de grammaire ainsi que le vocabulaire en fin d'ouvrage, traduire, puis corriger chaque page des exercices suivants :

1 - Ils nous connaissent.

2 - Je sais qu'il est avec toi.

3 - Leur mère veut travailler.

4 - Mon cousin travaille ici.

5 - J'aime les rencontrer ici.

6 - Elle préfère travailler ici.

7 - Vos enfants sont avec lui.

8 - Ils veulent notre voiture.

9 - Nous travaillons avec elle.

10 - Vous aimez notre amie.

11 - Elle connaît leur cousine.

12 - Elles sont avec mon père.

13 - Je préfère leurs amis.

14 - Nous vivons avec eux.

15 - Son fils est avec nos amis.

16 - Leur maison est à Watford.

17 - J'ai leur nouvelle adresse.

18 - Ma tante travaille à Hull.

19 - Je les rencontre à Oxford.

20 - Ils veulent travailler avec moi.

1 - They know us.

2 - I know he is with you.

3 - Their mother wants to work.

4 - My cousin works here.

5 - I like to meet them here.

6 - She prefers to work here.

7 - Your children are with him.

8 - They want our car.

9 - We work with her.

10 - You like (You love) our friend.

11 - She knows their cousin.

12 - They are with my father.

13 - I prefer their friends.

14 - We live with them.

15 - His/Her son is with our friends.

16 - Their house is in Watford.

17 - I have (I've got) their new address.

18 - My aunt works in Hull.

19 - I meet them in Oxford.

20 - They want to work with me.

1 - Nous habitons ici avec lui.
2 - John aime leur voiture.
3 - Elle sait que je suis ici.
4 - Notre nouvelle maison est ici.
5 - Mes amis sont avec toi.
6 - J'ai une cousine à Londres.
7 - Il a sa nouvelle voiture.
8 - Je connais leur nouvel ami.
9 - Tu connais notre frère.
10 - Nos amis habitent ici.
11 - Leur oncle vit en France.
12 - Je veux vivre en Angleterre.
13 - Je sais qu'ils sont ici.
14 - Elle sait qu'il est avec moi.
15 - Nous les rencontrons ici.
16 - Je sais qu'il aime être avec toi.
17 – Elles sont ici avec nous
18 - Ils connaissent ma sœur.
19 - Leurs enfants nous aiment.
20 - Ta sœur préfère notre maison.

1 - We live here with him.

2 - John likes their car.

3 - She knows I am here.

4 - Our new house is here.

5 - My friends are with you.

6 - I have (I've got) a cousin in London.

7 - He has (He's got) his new car.

8 - I know their new friend.

9 - You know our brother.

10 - Our friends live here.

11 - Their uncle lives in France.

12 - I want to live in England.

13 - I know they are here.

14 - She knows he is with me.

15 - We meet them here.

16 – I know he likes to be with you.

17 – They are here with us.

18 - They know my sister.

19 - Their children love (like) us.

20 - Your sister prefers our house.

1 - Nous travaillons à Paris.

2 - Leur fils est mon ami.

3 - Il connaît notre maison.

4 - Ils habitent avec elle à Oxford.

5 - Il veut me rencontrer ici.

6 - Sa mère travaille avec lui.

7 - J'aime ta nouvelle voiture.

8 - Notre amie travaille avec eux.

9 - Ils se rencontrent à Cork.

10 - Vous connaissez leur fils.

11 - Mon appartement est ici.

12 - Il sait que je préfère sa voiture.

13 - Nous sommes leurs amis.

14 - Ils préfèrent vivre à Cork.

15 - Mon frère vous connaît.

16 - Elle veut nous rencontrer ici.

17 - Vous aimez notre voiture.

18 - J'aime être ici avec eux.

19 - Elle le rencontre à Leeds.

20 - Leurs enfants sont avec elle.

1 - We work in Paris.

2 - Their son is my friend.

3 - He knows our house.

4 - They live with her in Oxford.

5 - He wants to meet me here.

6 - His mother works with him.

7 - I like your new car.

8 - Our friend works with them.

9 - They meet in Cork.

10 - You know their son.

11 - My flat is here.

12 - He knows I prefer his car.

13 - We are their friends.

14 - They prefer to live in Cork.

15 - My brother knows you.

16 - She wants to meet us here.

17 - You like our car.

18 - I like to be here with them.

19 - She meets him in Leeds.

20 - Their children are with her.

1 - Je préfère leurs enfants.

2 - Je les rencontre avec toi.

3 - Nous avons leur adresse.

4 - Mon cousin connaît leur fils.

5 - Elle aime notre maison.

6 - Ta tante est notre amie.

7 - Ils préfèrent être avec toi.

8 - Je sais qu'ils travaillent ici.

9 - Ils sont avec elle à Leeds.

10 - Mon cousin est ici avec eux.

11 - Ta sœur travaille avec lui.

12 - Elle veut travailler avec nous.

13 - Elles habitent ici avec moi.

14 - Je sais qu'ils sont avec toi.

15 - Ils nous rencontrent ici.

16 - Ma sœur est leur nouvelle amie.

17 - Je préfère les rencontrer ici.

18 - Il aime nous rencontrer avec toi.

19 - Je sais que tu les aimes.

20 - Ils connaissent notre adresse.

1 - I prefer their children.

2 - I meet them with you.

3 - We have (We've got) their address.

4 - My cousin knows their son.

5 - She likes our house.

6 - Your aunt is our friend.

7 - They prefer to be with you.

8 - I know they work here.

9 - They are with her in Leeds.

10 - My cousin is here with them.

11 - Your sister works with him.

12 - She wants to work with us.

13 - They live here with me.

14 - I know they are with you.

15 - They meet us here.

16 - My sister is their new friend.

17 - I prefer to meet them here.

18 - He likes to meet us with you.

19 - I know you love them (you like them).

20 - They know our address.

1 - Mes parents sont leurs amis.
2 - Ils ont une nouvelle voiture.
3 - Je suis à Bristol avec elle.
4 - J'ai trois maisons en France.
5 - Jonathan est notre cousin.
6 - Nous sommes vos amis.
7 - Ils ont un nouvel appartement.
8 - Leur nouvelle adresse est ici.
9 - Elle est en France avec eux.
10 - Leur ami est notre cousin.
11 - Ton oncle a deux frères.
12 - J'ai trois amis à Birmingham.
13 - Ma mère a une tante à Paris.
14 - Nous sommes à Cork avec lui.
15 - Nos enfants sont avec ta sœur.
16 - Mon appartement est à Oxford.
17 - Sa nouvelle maison est ici.
18 - Je suis ici avec vos enfants.
19 - Leur fils a trois amis à Hull.
20 - Nous avons un nouvel ami ici.

1 - My parents are their friends.

2 - They have (They've got) a new car.

3 - I am in Bristol with her.

4 - I have (I've got) three houses in France.

5 - Jonathan is our cousin.

6 - We are your friends.

7 - They have (They've got) a new flat.

8 - Their new address is here.

9 - She is in France with them.

10 - Their friend is our cousin.

11 - Your uncle has (has got) two brothers.

12 - I have (I've got) three friends in Birmingham.

13 - My mother has (has got) an aunt in Paris.

14 - We are in Cork with him.

15 - Our children are with your sister.

16 - My flat is in Oxford.

17 - His / Her new house is here.

18 - I am (I'm) here with your children.

19 - Their son has (has got) three friends in Hull.

20 - We have (We've got) a new friend here.

1 - Elles sont avec nous à Paris.

2 - Vos parents ont leur voiture.

3 - Ma tante est avec eux à Leeds.

4 - J'ai trois frères et deux sœurs.

5 - Il a une nouvelle amie anglaise.

6 - Nous sommes avec ton oncle.

7 - Ils ont une nouvelle adresse.

8 - Nos enfants sont avec nous.

9 - Nous avons une nouvelle voiture.

10 - Leur nouvelle maison est à Cork.

11 - J'ai un appartement à Leeds.

12 - Jane a un nouvel ami en France.

13 - Ils sont avec moi dans ta voiture.

14 - Mon père est leur ami.

15 - Notre oncle a votre voiture.

16 - Son appartement est à Liverpool.

17 - Elle a trois amies à Watford.

18 - Nos enfants sont leurs amis.

19 - Ils ont une nouvelle adresse ici.

20 - Elle est avec moi dans ma voiture.

1 - They are with us in Paris.

2 - Your parents have (have got) their car.

3 - My aunt is with them in Leeds.

4 - I have (I've got) three brothers and two sisters.

5 - He has (He's got) a new English friend.

6 - We are with your uncle.

7 - They have (They've got) a new address.

8 - Our children are with us.

9 - We have (We've got) a new car.

10 - Their new house is in Cork.

11 - I have (I've got) a flat in Leeds.

12 - Jane has (has got) a new friend in France.

13 - They are with me in your car.

14 - My father is their friend.

15 - Our uncle has (has got) your car.

16 - His / Her flat is in Liverpool.

17 - She has (She's got) three friends in Watford.

18 - Our children are their friends.

19 - They have (have got) a new address here.

20 - She is with me in my car.

1 - Leurs amis sont nos cousins.

2 - J'ai trois oncles et quatre tantes.

3 - Ma nouvelle maison est à Hull.

4 - Mes amis sont avec leurs enfants.

5 - Leur cousine est ici avec moi.

6 - Ses parents sont mes amis.

7 - Je suis avec eux dans ta maison.

8 - Ils ont une nouvelle adresse à Cork.

9 - Vous êtes leur ami et ils sont ici.

10 - Elle a mon adresse dans sa voiture.

11 - Leurs enfants sont ici avec nous.

12 - Il a notre adresse à Liverpool.

13 - Mes parents sont ici avec moi.

14 - Nous avons une nouvelle voiture.

15 - Tes amis sont nos cousins.

16 - Vous avez notre nouvelle adresse.

17 - Elle a trois oncles en Amérique.

18 - Mes amis sont avec elle à Paris.

19 - Leur frère a une nouvelle amie.

20 - Je suis avec eux dans ta voiture.

1 - Their friends are our cousins.

2 - I have (I've got) three uncles and four aunts.

3 - My new house is in Hull.

4 - My friends are with their children.

5 - Their cousin is here with me.

6 - His / Her parents are my friends.

7 - I am (I'm) with them in your house.

8 - They have (They've got) a new address in Cork.

9 - You are their friend and they are here.

10 - She has (She's got) my address in her car.

11 - Their children are here with us.

12 - He has (He's got) our address in Liverpool.

13 - My parents are here with me.

14 - We have (We've got) a new car.

15 - Your friends are our cousins.

16 - You have (You've got) our new address.

17 - She has (She's got) three uncles in America.

18 - My friends are with her in Paris.

19 - Their brother has (has got) a new friend.

20 - I am (I'm) with them in your car.

1 - Leurs enfants ont notre adresse.
2 - Votre amie anglaise est avec lui.
3 - Nous avons une nouvelle cousine.
4 - Kevin a notre adresse en France.
5 - Nos amis ont trois voitures.
6 - Tes enfants sont ici avec moi.
7 - Je suis avec eux dans ta maison.
8 - Votre nouvel appartement est ici.
9 - Il est mon ami et il a notre adresse.
10 - J'ai une nouvelle maison à Leeds.
11 - Mes parents ont quatre enfants.
12 - Nous avons leur nouvelle voiture.
13 - Tes amis sont avec nous à Paris.
14 - Ils ont trois nouveaux amis ici.
15 - Je suis avec elle dans ta voiture.
16 - Leurs enfants ont un oncle à Cork.
17 - Mon frère est ton nouvel ami.
18 - Elles sont à Liverpool avec nous.
19 - J'ai trois nouvelles amies à Leeds.
20 - Notre oncle est avec leur frère.

1 - Their children have (have got) our address.

2 - Your English friend is with him.

3 - We have (We've got) a new cousin.

4 - Kevin has (has got) our address in France.

5 - Our friends have (have got) three cars.

6 - Your children are here with me.

7 - I am (I'm) with them in your house.

8 - Your new flat is here.

9 - He is (He's) my friend and he has (he's got) our address.

10 - I have (I've got) a new house in Leeds.

11 - My parents have (have got) four children.

12 - We have (We've got) their new car.

13 - Your friends are with us in Paris.

14 - They have (They've got) three new friends here.

15 - I am (I'm) with her in your car.

16 - Their children have (have got) an uncle in Cork.

17 - My brother is your new friend.

18 - They are in Liverpool with us.

19 - I have (I've got) three new friends in Leeds.

20 - Our uncle is with their brother.

1 - Mes parents aiment ta voiture.

2 - Ta sœur veut rencontrer mon frère.

3 - Leurs cousins sont nos amis.

4 - Mon ami travaille avec ses parents.

5 - Nous la rencontrons avec sa sœur.

6 - Notre oncle est avec ton père.

7 - Leur fils rencontre mon frère ici.

8 - Nos enfants sont avec leur tante.

9 - Leurs amis travaillent avec mes cousins.

10 - Notre mère préfère ton fils.

11 - Mes parents aiment tes nouveaux amis.

12 - Sa sœur sait que je suis avec tes parents.

13 - Mon père a leur nouvelle adresse.

14 - Nos amis veulent rencontrer ton frère.

15 - Ses parents savent que je suis votre ami.

16 - Ton oncle vit avec notre cousine.

17 - Son frère veut rencontrer ta tante.

18 - Leurs parents savent tu es notre ami.

19 - Leur fils travaille avec mon oncle.

20 - Votre sœur connaît leur fille.

1 - My parents like your car.

2 - Your sister wants to meet my brother.

3 - Their cousins are our friends.

4 - My friend works with his parents.

5 - We meet her with her sister.

6 - Our uncle is with your father.

7 - Their son meets my brother here.

8 - Our children are with their aunt.

9 - Their friends work with my cousins.

10 - Our mother prefers your son.

11 - My parents like/love your new friends.

12 - His/Her sister knows I'm with your parents.

13 - My father has (has got) their new address.

14 - Our friends want to meet your brother.

15 - His/Her parents know I am your friend.

16 - Your uncle lives with our cousin.

17 - His/Her brother wants to meet your aunt.

18 - Their parents know you are our friend.

19 - Their son works with my uncle.

20 - Your sister knows their daughter.

1 - Mes amis veulent rencontrer ton frère.

2 - Nos parents savent que tu es avec leurs amis.

3 - Ma soeur préfère travailler avec son oncle.

4 - Notre cousin vit avec ses nouveaux amis.

5 - Sa mère rencontre nos amis à Leeds.

6 - Mon fils veut travailler avec ton père.

7 - Leurs cousins savent que j'aime ta sœur.

8 - Tes amis savent que leur voiture est ici.

9 - Notre oncle préfère être avec tes amis.

10 - Mon père a votre adresse dans sa voiture.

11 - Sa sœur sait que je préfère votre cousine.

12 - Leurs parents veulent rencontrer mon fils.

13 - Notre fils sait que ses amis sont ici.

14 - Nos amis sont dans leur voiture.

15 - Ta sœur veut rencontrer mes amis.

16 - Leurs parents savent que j'aime ton frère.

17 - Mes amis veulent travailler avec ton cousin.

18 - Notre oncle sait que je suis avec ses amis.

19 - Leurs enfants préfèrent être avec ma sœur.

20 - Tes amis veulent travailler avec notre père.

1 - My friends want to meet your brother.

2 - Our parents know you are with their friends.

3 - My sister prefers to work with her uncle.

4 - Our cousin lives with his new friends.

5 - His/Her mother meets our friends in Leeds.

6 - My son wants to work with your father.

7 - Their cousins know I like/love your sister.

8 - Your friends know their car is here.

9 - Our uncle prefers to be with your friends.

10 - My father has (has got) your address in his car.

11 - His/Her sister knows I prefer your cousin.

12 - Their parents want to meet my son.

13 - Our son knows his friends are here.

14 - Our friends are in their car.

15 - Your sister wants to meet my friends.

16 - Their parents know I love/like your brother.

17 - My friends want to work with your cousin.

18 - Our uncle knows I am with his friends.

19 - Their children prefer to be with my sister.

20 - Your friends want to work with our father.

1 - Notre fils est dans sa nouvelle voiture.
2 - Ma soeur préfère sa cousine Amy.
3 - Leur mère veut rencontrer notre père.
4 - Mon oncle sait que je préfère ta soeur.
5 - Elle rencontre ses amis dans ce restaurant.
6 – Je sais qu'il aime sa nouvelle voiture.
7 - Ma soeur rencontre ses amis à Liverpool.
8 - Leurs cousins préfèrent me rencontrer ici.
9 - Mon frère a sa nouvelle voiture.
10 - Notre tante veut travailler avec ton père.
11 - Mon fils est dans sa chambre avec eux.
12 - Notre cousine préfère être avec vos enfants.
13 - Elle veut venir ici avec ses amis.
14 - Mon ami vit ici avec ses parents.
15 - Ils ont leur nouvelle voiture française.
16 - Tes parents savent que ton frère m'aime.
17 - Ta voiture est dans son nouveau garage.
18 - Nos cousins aiment leur nouvelle maison.
19 - Ton amie préfère vivre avec mon frère.
20 - Mon fils sait que tes enfants sont ici.

1 - Our son is in his new car.

2 - My sister prefers her cousin Amy.

3 - Their mother wants to meet our father.

4 - My uncle knows I prefer your sister.

5 - She meets her friends in this/that restaurant.

6 - I know he likes his new car.

7 - My sister meets her friends in Liverpool.

8 - Their cousins prefer to meet me here.

9 - My brother has (got) his new car.

10 - Our aunt wants to work with your father.

11 - My son is in his (bed)room with them.

12 - Our cousin prefers to be with your children.

13 - She wants to come here with her friends.

14 - My friend lives here with his parents.

15 - They have (got) their new French car.

16 - Your parents know your brother loves/likes me.

17 - Your car is in its new garage.

18 - Our cousins like their new house.

19 - Your friend prefers to live with my brother.

20 - My son knows your children are here.

1 - Votre fils travaille ici avec ma sœur.

2 - Leurs enfants sont dans votre voiture.

3 - Elle préfère me rencontrer avec toi.

4 - Ils aiment leurs nouveaux amis.

5 - Mon cousin préfère sa nouvelle voiture.

6 - Vos amis savent que j'aime leur fille.

7 - Mon oncle vous rencontre à Coventry.

8 - Nos amis veulent travailler avec elle.

9 - Mon frère préfère être dans ta chambre.

10 - Elle aime sa nouvelle maison anglaise.

11 - Ta nouvelle voiture est dans mon garage.

12 - Sa cousine préfère notre appartement.

13 - Ta fille veut vivre avec ici avec mon fils.

14 - Nos amis rencontrent ta cousine ici.

15 - Elle préfère travailler avec ses amis.

16 - Il sait que sa sœur veut me rencontrer.

17 - Ma mère est ici avec tes parents.

18 - J'aime leur nouveau salon anglais.

19 - Votre tante sait que son fils est ici.

20 - Tes cousins travaillent avec mon frère.

1 - Your son works here with my sister.

2 - Their children are in your car.

3 - She prefers to meet me with you.

4 - They like/love their new friends.

5 - My cousin prefers his new car.

6 - Your friends know I love/like their daughter.

7 - My uncle meets you in Coventry.

8 - Our friends want to work with her.

9 - My brother prefers to be in your (bed)room.

10 - She likes her new English house.

11 - Your new car is in my garage.

12 - His/Her cousin prefers our flat.

13 - Your daughter wants to live here with my son.

14 - Our friends meet your cousin here.

15 - She prefers to work with her friends.

16 - He knows his sister wants to meet me.

17 - My mother is here with your parents.

18 - I like their new English living-room.

19 - Your aunt knows her son is here.

20 - Your cousins work with my brother.

Résumé Grammatical Etape 0/3

Le cas possessif :   (exemple : « La fille de Bob »).

Le cas possessif se construit en inversant les termes par rapport au français, en supprimant les articles « le », « la », « les » et « de », et en intercalant un «'s » entre les deux termes du rapport de possession. Tout ce qui est compris entre « le » ou « la » ou « les » et « de » bascule après le terme du possesseur :

La voiture **de** Bob = Bob's car
(comme si l'on disait « Bob's voiture » !)
La nouvelle voiture italienne **de** Bob = Bob's new Italian car.

Lorsque le nom du possesseur est précédé par « du », « de la » ou « des », (à la place de « de »), il reste l'article « the » en début d'expression :

La voiture **du** directeur = **The** manager's car.
(puisque « du » = « de le » et « de » disparaît. Reste « **le** »)
La voiture **de la** secrétaire = **The** secretary's car.
(même logique : « de » disparaît, in ne reste plus que « **la** »)
La voiture **des** Wilson = **The** Wilsons'car.
(puisque « des » = « de les » et « de » disparaît. Reste « **les** »)
(On remarque que les noms de famille doivent se mettre au pluriel en parlant du couple ou de la famille)

« De » devant chaque fois disparaître, reste alors « le », « la » ou « les » = **the**

Autrement dit, il n'y a **aucun article** en anglais que lorsque le terme du possesseur est précédé par « **de** » en français.

Dans le cas d'un pluriel en « s », on n'ajoute que l'apostrophe (par écrit) sans le « s » du cas possessif :

La voiture **des** Miller = The Miller<u>s'</u> car.

Mais un second « s » (possessif) est nécessaire en cas de mot singulier se terminant déjà par un « s » :

La voiture de Jame<u>s</u> = Jame<u>**'s**</u> car.   (A prononcer « Jeïmziz Kâââ »)

En utilisant ces éléments de grammaire ainsi que le vocabulaire en fin d'ouvrage, traduire, puis corriger chaque page des exercices suivants :

1 - Je sais qu'il est le frère de Jonathan.

2 - La voiture de Christopher est ici.

3 - J'ai l'adresse de leurs parents.

4 - Nos amis sont dans la voiture de Jack.

5 - La maison de Bob est à Liverpool.

6 - J'ai la nouvelle adresse de Steve.

7 - La sœur de Linda veut nous rencontrer.

8 - Je préfère la maison de tes parents.

9 - L'amie de mon frère habite à Leeds.

10 - La tante de Jim veut travailler ici.

11 - La maison de William est en Angleterre.

12 - Elle travaille avec le cousin de Jill.

13 - Je connais l'appartement de Mark.

14 - Il aime être avec les enfants de Pat.

15 - Elle sait que la voiture de Jim est ici.

16 - C'est la nouvelle maison des Spencer.

17 - J'ai la nouvelle adresse de William.

18 - Je connais le frère de Margaret.

19 - Il préfère travailler avec l'ami d'Edgar.

20 - Nous sommes avec les sœurs d'Andrew.

1 - I know he is Jonathan's brother.

2 - Christopher's car is here.

3 - I have (I've got) their parents' address.

4 - Our friends are in Jack's car.

5 - Bob's house is in Liverpool.

6 - I have (I've got) Steve's new address.

7 - Linda's sister wants to meet us.

8 - I prefer your parents' house.

9 - My brother's friend lives in Leeds.

10 - Jim's aunt wants to work here.

11 - William's house is in England.

12 - She works with Jill's cousin.

13 - I know Mark's flat.

14 - He likes to be with Pat's children.

15 - She knows Jim's car is here.

16 - It/This/That is the Spencers' new house.

17 - I have (I've got) William's new address.

18 - I know Margaret's brother.

19 - He prefers to work with Edgar's friend.

20 - We are with Andrew's sisters.

1 - Je préfère travailler avec le cousin de Jo.

2 - Ils rencontrent les parents de Kate ici.

3 - Le frère de ton père est ton oncle.

4 - La tante de Jill est la sœur de sa mère.

5 - Il veut rencontrer les cousins de Bernie.

6 - Cette fille est l'amie de ma sœur.

7 - Je sais que ce garçon est le frère de Jill.

8 - Nous avons l'adresse des Flint à Hull.

9 - C'est le nouvel appartement de Linda.

10 - Fiona connaît le nouvel ami de Steve.

11 - L'adresse de ta sœur est dans ma voiture.

12 - Ces enfants sont les cousins de ton ami.

13 - Mon père habite dans la maison de Tony.

14 - Ils aiment être avec les cousins de John.

15 - Je sais qu'il travaille avec l'ami de Pat.

16 - La nouvelle voiture des Parker est ici.

17 - Je connais l'adresse de vos parents.

18 - Je vis avec les cousins de votre sœur.

19 - Les amis de ta mère sont à Liverpool.

20 - Je sais qu'il est avec le cousin d'Andy.

1 - I prefer to work with Jo's cousin.

2 - They meet Kate's parents here.

3 - Your father's brother is your uncle.

4 - Jill's aunt is her mother's sister.

5 - He wants to meet Bernie's cousins.

6 - This/That girl is my sister's friend.

7 - I know this/that boy is Jill's brother.

8 - We have (We've got) the Flints' address in Hull.

9 - It/This/That is Linda's new flat.

10 - Fiona knows Steve's new friend.

11 - Your sister's address is in my car.

12 - These children are your friend's cousins.

13 - My father lives in Tony's house.

14 - They like to be with John's cousins.

15 - I know he works with Pat's friend.

16 - The Parkers' new car is here.

17 - I know your parents' address.

18 - I live with your sister's cousins.

19 - Your mother's friends are in Liverpool.

20 - I know he is with Andy's cousin.

1 - Il aime rencontrer les amis de Steven.

2 - La voiture de vos parents est à Leeds.

3 - C'est la nouvelle maison des Wilson.

4 - Je préfère travailler avec l'ami de Jo.

5 - La tante d'Amy a une nouvelle adresse.

6 - C'est l'appartement de tes cousins.

7 - Je veux travailler avec le père de Sam.

8 - Audrey sait que j'aime l'ami d'Arthur.

9 - Ces enfants sont les amis de Bill.

10 - C'est la nouvelle voiture de ma mère.

11 - Le frère de Jo veut travailler avec moi.

12 - Les parents de Mark sont avec nous.

13 - Je connais le père de votre cousine.

14 - Leur fils est le nouvel ami de Jenny.

15 - J'aime être avec les cousins de William.

16 - Je préfère rencontrer l'ami de Bob ici.

17 - Je sais qu'ils sont avec les frères de Jane.

18 - La sœur de Jim est ma nouvelle amie.

19 - Le père de Bob nous rencontre à Cork.

20 - Linda est la nouvelle amie de ma sœur.

1 - He likes to meet Steven's friends.

2 - Your parents' car is in Leeds.

3 - It/This/That is the Wilsons' new house.

4 - I prefer to work with Jo's friend.

5 - Amy's aunt has (has got) a new address.

6 - It/This/That is your cousins' flat.

7 - I want to work with Sam's father.

8 - Audrey knows I love (I like) Arthur's friend.

9 - These children are Bill's friends.

10 - It/This/That is my mother's new car.

11 - Jo's brother wants to work with me.

12 - Mark's parents are with us.

13 - I know your cousin's father.

14 - Their son is Jenny's new friend.

15 - I like to be with William's cousins.

16 - I prefer to meet Bob's friend here.

17 - I know they are (they're) with Jane's brothers.

18 - Jim's sister is my new friend.

19 - Bob's father meets us in Cork.

20 - Linda is my sister's new friend.

1 - Je veux rencontrer les amis des Wilson.

2 - Ces enfants sont les cousins de Malcolm.

3 - La tante de William travaille avec nous.

4 - Nous sommes les nouveaux amis de Jo.

5 - Je préfère être avec les parents de Jack.

6 - Elle vit ici avec les cousins de ton père.

7 - L'ami des Wilson veut te rencontrer ici.

8 - Je sais qu'ils sont les parents de Kevin.

9 - C'est la nouvelle adresse de ma sœur.

10 - La maison des Spencer est à New-York.

11 - Ces enfants sont les frères de ton amie.

12 - Je connais les parents de ta cousine.

13 - Elle aime travailler avec l'oncle de Sam.

14 - Je sais qu'il préfère la voiture des Fox.

15 - Ils ont la nouvelle adresse de ton père.

16 - La nouvelle maison de Jo est à Brighton.

17 - Elle travaille avec les amis de ma mère.

18 - Ils savent que la cousine de Mary est ici.

19 - Leurs enfants sont avec l'amie de Stan.

20 - C'est la nouvelle voiture de ton frère.

1 - I want to meet the Wilsons' friends.

2 - These children are Malcolm's cousins.

3 - William's aunt works with us.

4 - We are Jo's new friends.

5 - I prefer to be with Jack's parents.

6 - She lives here with your father's cousins.

7 - The Wilsons' friend wants to meet you here.

8 - I know they are Kevin's parents.

9 - It/This/That is my sister's new address.

10 - The Spencers' house is in New-York

11 - These children are your friend's brothers.

12 - I know your cousin's parents.

13 - She likes to work with Sam's uncle.

14 - I know he prefers the Foxes' car.

15 - They have (They've got) your father's new address.

16 - Jo's new house is in Brighton.

17 - She works with my mother's friends.

18 - They know Mary's cousin is here.

19 - Their children are with Stan's friend.

20 - It/This/That is your brother's new car.

1 - Je connais les enfants de Mme Parker.

2 - Les amis de Bob sont avec notre fils.

3 - Elles veulent travailler avec la fille de Stan.

4 - Je sais que la cousine de Bob habite ici.

5 - La nouvelle adresse de Jack est à Hull.

6 - Ces filles sont les nouvelles amies de Jill.

7 - Le frère de Pat préfère me rencontrer ici.

8 - Cette femme est l'amie de notre cousin.

9 - Le fils d'Andrew veut travailler à Leeds.

10 - Ce jeune garçon est le neveu de William.

11 - Les parents de vos amis sont dans le jardin.

12 - Il veut te rencontrer avec la soeur de Glen.

13 - Nous savons que la nièce de Jane habite ici.

14 - Elle préfère travailler avec les amis de Chris.

15 - Le nouvel appartement de James est à Watford.

16 - Elle sait que je préfère la maison des Wilson.

17 - Ils sont avec nous dans le restaurant de Bernie.

18 - Les cousins de Jo préfèrent travailler avec moi.

19 - Nous savons qu'il est avec les neveux de Bob.

20 - La voiture des Flint est dans notre garage.

1 - I know Mrs Parker's children.

2 - Bob's friends are with our son.

3 - They want to work with Stan's daughter.

4 - I know Bob's cousin lives here.

5 - Jack's new address is in Hull.

6 - These girls are Jill's new friends.

7 - Pat's brother prefers to meet me here.

8 - This/That woman is our cousin's friend.

9 - Andrew's son wants to work in Leeds.

10 - This/That young boy is William's nephew.

11 - Your friends' parents are in the garden.

12 - He wants to meet you with Glen's sister.

13 - We know Jane's niece lives here.

14 - She prefers to work with Chris's friends

15 - James's new flat is in Watford.

16 - She knows I prefer the Wilsons' new house.

17 - They are with us in Bernie's restaurant.

18 - Jo's cousins prefer to work with me.

19 - We know he is with Bob's nephews.

20 - The Flints' car is in our garage.

1 - Les Parker aiment le nouvel appartement de Stan.

2 - Le frère de Kelly veut travailler ici avec nous.

3 - Mark veut rencontrer les amis de Christopher.

4 - Elle sait que nous sommes avec les amis de Jim.

5 - Nous aimons la nouvelle chambre de Jenny.

6 - Les cousins de Malcolm préfèrent être avec nous.

7 - Cette jeune fille est la nièce de Mme Baldwin.

8 - Le père de John sait que tu as ta voiture.

9 - Ces gens sont les nouveaux amis de mon oncle.

10 - Il sait que la maison des Spencer est à Hull.

11 - Le neveu de Bill préfère nous rencontrer ici.

12 - Je rencontre les amis de mon frère à Londres.

13 - Il sait que j'aime le nouveau jardin de vos cousins.

14 - Les nouveaux amis anglais de Bob sont avec moi.

15 - Le fils de Mr. Brown aime ces vieilles maisons.

16 - Je préfère la nouvelle voiture de Linda.

17 - Ils veulent connaître la nouvelle adresse de Karl.

18 - Je sais que vous rencontrez l'oncle de mon amie.

19 - Tu préfères travailler avec les cousins des Parker.

20 - Je sais que c'est la nouvelle chambre de Betty.

1 - The Parkers like Stan's new flat.

2 - Kelly's brother wants to work here with us.

3 - Mark wants to meet Christopher's friends.

4 - She knows we are with Jim's friends.

5 - We like Jenny's new (bed)room.

6 - Malcolm's cousins prefer to be with us.

7 - This/That young girl is Mrs Baldwin's niece.

8 - John's father knows you have (you've got) your car.

9 - These people are my uncle's new friends.

10 - He knows the Spencers' house is in Hull.

11 - Bill's nephew prefers to meet us here.

12 - I meet my brother's friends in London.

13 - He knows I like your cousins' new garden

14 - Bob's new English friends are with me.

15 - Mr. Brown's son likes these old houses.

16 - I prefer Linda's new car.

17 - They want to know Karl's new address.

18 - I know you meet my friend's uncle.

19 - You prefer to work with the Parkers' cousins.

20 - I know it/this/that is Betty's new (bed)room.

1 - Elle sait que j'aime le frère de Barbara.
2 - Notre cousine travaille avec l'ami de Mark.
3 - C'est le nouvel appartement des Spencer.
4 - Je sais que leur fille est la nièce de M. Fox.
5 - Il préfère venir avec la soeur de Mike.
6 - J'aime la nouvelle chambre de ton frère.
7 - Ces gens veulent rencontrer l'ami de Jo.
8 - Ils sont dans le jardin de vos parents.
9 - Le neveu de M. Young travaille avec moi.
10 - Je préfère aller à Cork avec la soeur de Jim.
11 - Cette femme est la nouvelle amie de Sarah.
12 - Les nouveaux amis de Jack vivent à Paris.
13 - Cette jeune fille est la cousine des Parker.
14 - Nous voulons rencontrer les parents de Jill.
15 – Ton frère est dans la voiture de nos amis.
16 - Je sais qu'il aime le nouveau jardin d'Edgar.
17 - Elle connaît l'adresse de votre fils à Leeds.
18 - Ces enfants sont les nouveaux amis de Bob.
19 - Tu sais que je préfère les amis français de Jim.
20 - C'est le nouveau restaurant de vos parents.

1 - She knows I love (I like) Barbara's brother.

2 - Our cousin works with Mark's friend.

3 - It/This/That is the Spencers' new flat.

4 - I know their daughter is Mr. Fox's niece.

5 - He prefers to come with Mike's sister.

6 - I like your brother's new (bed)room.

7 - These people want to meet Jo's friend.

8 - They are in your parents' garden.

9 - Mr Young's nephew works with me.

10 - I prefer to go to Cork with Jim's sister.

11 - This/That woman is Sarah's new friend.

12 - Jack's new friends live in Paris.

13 - This/That young girl is the Parkers' cousin.

14 - We want to meet Jill's parents.

15 – Your brother is in our friends' car.

16 - I know he likes Edgar's new garden.

17 - She knows your son's address in Leeds.

18 - These children are Bob's new friends.

19 - You know I prefer Jim's French friends.

20 - It/This/That is your parents' new restaurant.

1 - Leur tante travaille avec la sœur d'Alice.

2 - Les cousins de Jill préfèrent notre maison.

3 - Je sais que l'ami de Steve habite à Hull.

4 - J'aime la nouvelle maison des Spencer.

5 - Le frère de Betty est dans la salle de bain.

6 - Je connais la nouvelle chambre de Pat.

7 - Cet enfant est avec les amis de mon fils.

8 - Les parents de Bob veulent te rencontrer.

9 - Ils savent que j'aime la fille de Steven.

10 - Ces gens sont les amis français de Mark.

11 - Je préfère la nouvelle voiture des Lawson.

12 - Il sait que la mère de mon ami est anglaise.

13 - Le neveu de Jo travaille avec ces gens.

14 - Ce jeune garçon est l'ami de notre fils.

15 - Ils ont la nouvelle adresse de Pat à Hull.

16 - Sue préfère travailler avec l'ami de ton fils.

17 - Ces enfants sont les cousins de Mme Glen.

18 - La fille de Sarah veut travailler avec toi.

19 - Ils ont une nouvelle voiture française.

20 - Je préfère les rencontrer avec l'ami de Jo.

1 - Their aunt works with Alice's sister.

2 - Jill's cousins prefer our house.

3 - I know Steve's friend lives in Hull.

4 - I like the Spencers' new house.

5 - Betty's brother is in the bathroom.

6 - I know Pat's new (bed)room.

7 - This child is with my son's friends.

8 - Bob's parents want to meet you.

9 - They know I love/like Steven's daughter.

10 - These people are Mark's French friends.

11 - I prefer the Lawsons' new car.

12 - He knows my friend's mother is English.

13 - Jo's nephew works with these people.

14 - This young boy is our son's friend.

15 - They have (got) Pat's new address in Hull.

16 - Sue prefers to work with your son's friend.

17 - These children are Mrs Glen's cousins.

18 - Sarah's daughter wants to work with you.

19 - They have (got) a new French car.

20 - I prefer to meet them with Jo's friend.

1 - La soeur de Kate est dans notre cuisine.

2 - J'aime la nouvelle salle de bain de Jo.

3 - Je sais qu'ils sont avec les enfants de Pat.

4 - L'ami de Paul préfère venir avec moi.

5 - Je le rencontre dans le restaurant de Jill.

6 - Cette voiture est pour le neveu de Harry.

7 - La nouvelle adresse de Pat est à Leeds.

8 - Les parents de mon ami sont en France.

9 - La soeur de Jo veut me rencontrer ici.

10 - Il sait que je préfère la maison de Jack.

11 - Cette fille est la nouvelle amie de Mary.

12 - Il connaît les nouveaux amis de Mike.

13 - Mon père travaille avec l'oncle de Joe.

14 - Les fils de Jane veulent venir avec toi.

15 - La nouvelle voiture d'Andy est ici.

16 - Les enfants de Kim sont dans le garage.

17 - Il préfère être avec les cousins de Sue.

18 - Ce jeune homme est le nouvel ami de Jo.

19 - Le père de mon ami veut habiter ici.

20 - Ces gens sont les cousins de mon amie.

1 - Kate's sister is in our kitchen.

2 - I like Jo's new bathroom.

3 - I know they are with Pat's children.

4 - Paul's friend prefers to come with me.

5 - I meet him in Jill's restaurant.

6 - This/That car is for Harry's nephew.

7 - Pat's new address is in Leeds.

8 - My friend's parents are in France.

9 - Jo's sister wants to meet me here.

10 - He knows I prefer Jack's house.

11 - This/That girl is Mary's new friend.

12 - He knows Mike's new friends.

13 - My father works with Joe's uncle.

14 - Jane's sons want to come with you.

15 - Andy's new car is here.

16 - Kim's children are in the garage.

17 - He prefers to be with Sue's cousins.

18 - This/That young man is Jo's new friend.

19 - My friend's father wants to live here.

20 - These people are my friend's cousins.

1 - La nouvelle amie de Mark vit à Paris.

2 - Il sait que le neveu de John est ici.

3 - Cette fille est la nièce de M. Parker.

4 - Nous sommes avec les enfants de Jo.

5 - C'est le nouvel appartement de Kim.

6 - Il veut l'adresse de ton père à Cork.

7 - Ces gens sont les cousins de ton amie.

8 - J'aime la nouvelle maison de ton frère.

9 - Les amis Français de Bob sont avec lui.

10 - Il sait que je vis avec l'amie de sa soeur.

11 - Cet homme est l'oncle de Mme Flint.

12 - Je préfère rencontrer les amis de Jenny.

13 - Leur mère sait que le frère de Jo est ici.

14 - Ils sont avec moi dans la voiture de John.

15 - La tante de Jack est dans notre salon.

16 - Je préfère travailler avec les amis d'Anna.

17 - Il connaît la nouvelle adresse de Steve.

18 - Mike préfère être avec le fils d'Andrew.

19 - C'est la nouvelle chambre de nos parents.

20 - Je sais que les amis des Flint sont Anglais.

1 - Mark's new friend lives in Paris.

2 - He knows John's nephew is here.

3 - This/That girl is Mr. Parker's niece.

4 - We are with Jo's children.

5 - It/This/That is Kim's new flat.

6 - He wants your father's address in Cork.

7 - These people are your friend's cousins.

8 - I like your brother's new house.

9 - Bob's French friends are with him.

10 - He knows I live with his sister's friend.

11 - This/That man is Mrs Flint's uncle.

12 - I prefer to meet Jenny's friends.

13 - Their mother knows Jo's brother is here.

14 - They are with me in John's car.

15 - Jack's aunt is in our living-room.

16 - I prefer to work with Anna's friends.

17 - He knows Steve's new address.

18 - Mike prefers to be with Andrew's son.

19 - It/This/That is our parents' new (bed)room.

20 - I know the Flints' friends are English.

1 - La nouvelle amie de mon frère vit ici.

2 - Ce garçon est le fils de M. Wilkinson.

3 - Judith aime le jardin de vos parents.

4 - Les cousins de Pat veulent te rencontrer.

5 - Le nouveau restaurant de Jim est à Paris.

6 - Je suis avec eux dans la voiture de Bob.

7 - Ces gens préfèrent la maison de ta soeur.

8 - Il travaille avec le neveu de Mme Flint.

9 - La soeur de Betty veut vivre en France.

10 - Je préfère rencontrer les amis de Jim ici.

11 – Il connaît les nouveaux amis de Jo.

12 - Le frère de Jill est dans la chambre d'Anna.

13 - Elle sait que les amis d'Henry sont ici.

14 - C'est la nouvelle voiture anglaise de Jim.

15 - Les cousins de William sont avec nous.

16 - Cette femme connaît l'adresse des Parker.

17 - Le garage des Walker est pour ta voiture.

18 - Les parents de mon ami travaillent à Cork.

19 - Il veut rencontrer les cousins de Maggie.

20 - Cet homme connaît l'adresse de ton oncle.

1 - My brother's new (girl)friend lives here.

2 - This/That boy is Mr. Wilkinson's son.

3 - Judith likes your parents' garden.

4 - Pat's cousins want to meet you.

5 - Jim's new restaurant is in Paris.

6 - I am with them in Bob's car.

7 - These people prefer your sister's house.

8 - He works with Mrs. Flint's nephew.

9 - Betty's sister wants to live in France.

10 - I prefer to meet Jim's friends here.

11 - He knows Jo's new friends.

12 - Jill's brother is in Anna's (bed)room.

13 - She knows Henry's friends are here.

14 - It/This/That is Jim's new English car.

15 - William's cousins are with us.

16 - This/That woman knows the Parkers' address.

17 - The Walker's garage is for your car.

18 - My friend's parents work in Cork.

19 - He wants to meet Maggie's cousins.

20 - This/That man knows your uncle's address.

1 - Tom préfère être dans la voiture de Paul.

2 - Les enfants de Jim sont avec mon neveu.

3 - Je connais la nouvelle adresse des Stone.

4 - Notre voiture est dans le garage de Jack.

5 - Elle veut vivre avec le frère de ton ami.

6 - L'oncle de Sam travaille ici avec nous.

7 - C'est la nouvelle voiture anglaise de Jo.

8 - Je sais qu'ils sont les amis de ta nièce.

9 - Le fils de Jane veut aller à New-York.

10 - Elle préfère travailler avec le neveu de Bob.

11 - La nouvelle maison de Ted est à Leeds.

12 - C'est l'adresse de vos amis à Hull.

13 - Ces gens préfèrent l'appartement des Fox.

14 - Nous sommes avec la soeur de ton ami.

15 - Il veut connaître l'adresse de ta cousine.

16 - Ta fille est dans le garage des Brown.

17 - La nouvelle adresse de Kevin est ici.

18 - Elle sait que la mère de Bill vit à Cork.

19 - J'aime la nouvelle chambre de Betty.

20 - Je rencontre les amis de Stan à Watford.

1 - Tom prefers to be in Paul's car.

2 - Jim's children are with my nephew.

3 - I know the Stones' new address.

4 - Our car is in Jack's garage.

5 - She wants to live with your friend's brother.

6 - Sam's uncle works here with us.

7 - It/This/That is Jo's new English car.

8 - I know they are your niece's friends.

9 - Jane's son wants to go to New-York.

10 - She prefers to work with Bob's nephew.

11 - Ted's new house is in Leeds.

12 - It/This/That is your friends' address in Hull.

13 - These people prefer the Foxes' flat.

14 - We are with your friend's sister.

15 - He wants to know your cousin's address.

16 - Your daughter is in the Browns' garage.

17 - Kevin's new address is here.

18 - She knows Bill's mother lives in Cork.

19 - I like Betty's new (bed)room.

20 - I meet Stan's friends in Watford.

Résumé Grammatical Etape 0/4

1) Formes interrogative et négative dans le cas du **verbe « ETRE » (to be)** :

Appliquer le modèle suivant en conjuguant selon la personne concernée :

Affirmatif	Interrogatif	Négatif
Betty **is** English.	**Is** Betty English?	Betty **isn't** English.
They **are** here.	**Are** they here?	They **aren't** here.
		(Prononcer « hante »)

2) Formes interrogative et négative dans le cas de **tout AUTRE VERBE (seul)** :

Appliquer le modèle suivant en utilisant l'auxiliaire « to do » (faire) qui dans ce cas ne signifie rien en lui-même, tout comme le verbe être en français dans la formule « est-ce que » :

Affirmatif	Interrogatif	Négatif
She live**s** here.	**Does** she live here?	She **doesn't** live here.
	Prononcer « Daz »	(Pron. « Dazeunt' »)
They work here.	**Do** they work here?	They **don't** work here.

(To do = faire : I do, you do, he/she/it **does**, we do, you do, they do).

On remarque au passage que le "s" de la troisième personne s'applique alors à l'auxiliaire, et non plus au verbe qui redevient infinitif invariable (sans "to")

Autrement dit, quand un verbe quelconque est seul, il se conjugue en fonction de la troisième personne, mais si un auxiliaire l'accompagne, c'est ce dernier qui prend le « s » de conjugaison.

3) <u>Formes interrogative et négative dans le cas d'une GROUPE VERBAL COMPOSE</u>, c'est-à-dire d'un verbe précédé d'un autre verbe servant d'auxilaire comme dans le cas de la formule « **have got** », ainsi qu'avec « **can** » ou « **must** » :

Le verbe "to have" (avoir) se transforme comme n'importe quel verbe normal (donc avec « do ») **sauf** lorsqu'il accompagne un autre verbe, comme dans la formule idiomatique « **have got** » où « have » tient lieu d'auxiliaire et remplace alors « do » pour transformer (comme tout autre auxiliaire déjà présent à l'affirmatif, tel que **can** (pouvoir) ou **must** (devoir), par exemple :

<u>Affirmatif</u>	<u>Interrogatif</u>	<u>Négatif</u>
He **has got** his car.	**Has** he **got** his car?	He **hasn't got** his car.
She **can** come.	**Can** she come?	She **can't** come.
(Pron. "canne")	(idem)	(Pron. "Kant")
You **must** phone.	**Must** you phone?	You **mustn't** phone.
(Pron. « mast »	(idem)	(Pron. « masseunt »)

En utilisant ces éléments de grammaire, transformer chaque phrase en écrivant les deux autres formes de la phrase proposée, puis corriger à chaque fin de page. Pour **bien identifier le verbe**, imaginer la phrase à l'affirmatif si elle n'y est pas déjà, puis appliquer le modèle correspondant. (Verbe être, tout autre verbe ou groupe verbal composé).

1 - Barbara is French.

2 - They have a new car.

3 - She works with you.

4 - They are with William.

5 - She's got a new car.

6 - They want to meet me.

7 - We are their friends.

8 - They've got our address.

9 - He works with them.

10 - She prefers your car.

11 - They are in the kitchen.

12 - You've got a new house.

13 - Mike's friends are here.

14 - They like our new house.

15 - These people are her friends.

16 - They want to live here.

17 - They've got a new flat.

18 - They know you are here.

19 - Sharon has two sisters.

20 - They've got a big garden.

1 - Is Barbara French? Barbara isn't French.
2 - Do they have a new car? They don't have a new car.
3 - Does she work with you? She doesn't work with you.
4 - Are they with William? They aren't with William.
5 - Has she got a new car? She hasn't got a new car.
6 - Do they want to meet me? They don't want to meet me.
7 - Are we their friends? We aren't their friends.
8 - Have they got our address? They haven't got our address.
9 - Does he work with them? He doesn't work with them.
10 - Does she prefer your car? She doesn't prefer your car.
11 - Are they in the kitchen? They aren't in the kitchen.
12 - Have you got a new house? You haven't got a new house.
13 - Are Mike's friends here? Mike's friends aren't here.
14 - Do they like our new house? They don't like our new house.
15 - Are these people her friends? These people aren't her friends.
16 - Do they want to live here? They don't want to live here.
17 - Have they got a new flat? They haven't got a new flat.
18 - Do they know you are here? They don't know you are here.
19 - Does Sharon have two sisters? Sharon doesn't have two sisters.
20 - Have they got a big garden? They haven't got a big garden.

1 - Their house is very old.

2 - This garage is for Jim's car.

3 - Henry's parents work here.

4 - She wants to meet you.

5 - They are with our sister.

6 - He knows I love you.

7 - They are here to meet you.

8 - Alison wants this car.

9 - She knows Kevin's brother.

10 - These people are Jo's friends.

11 - They work with our uncle.

12 - She's got a new boyfriend.

13 - These people live here.

14 - Jack's car is in its garage.

15 - They meet in this restaurant.

16 - They are Wendy's friends.

17 - She knows that boy.

18 - They want to work with me.

19 - We've got Jo's new address.

20 - Their daughter works in Hull.

1 - Is their house very old? Their house isn't very old.
2 - Is this garage for Jim's car? This garage isn't for Jim's car.
3 - Do Henry's parents work here? Henry's parents don't work here.
4 - Does she want to meet you? She doesn't want to meet you.
5 - Are they with our sister? They aren't with our sister.
6 - Does he know I love you? He doesn't know I love you.
7 - Are they here to meet you? They aren't here to meet you.
8 - Does Alison want this car? Alison doesn't want this car.
9 - Does she know Kevin's brother? She doesn't know Kevin's brother.
10 - Are these people Jo's friends? These people aren't Jo's friends.
11 - Do they work with our uncle? They don't work with our uncle.
12 - Has she got a new boyfriend? She hasn't got a new boyfriend.
13 - Do these people live here? These people don't live here.
14 - Is Jack's car in its garage? Jack's car isn't in its garage.
15 - Do they meet in this restaurant? They don't meet in this restaurant.
16 - Are they Wendy's friends? They aren't Wendy's friends.
17 - Does she know that boy? She doesn't know that boy.
18 - Do they want to work with me? They don't want to work with me.
19 - Have we got Jo's new address. We haven't got Jo's new address.
20 - Does their daughter work in Hull? Their daughter doesn't work in Hull.

1 - Have they got our address?

2 - She doesn't work with you.

3 - They are with our sons.

4 - She doesn't know my name.

5 - You have your new car.

6 - Are these people your friends?

7 - Betty works with us.

8 - You've got a new car.

9 - The Wilsons are in Glasgow.

10 - She doesn't know I'm here.

11 - We work with their son.

12 - He's got our new address.

13 - The Spencers have this house.

14 - Jenny isn't in the garage.

15 - He doesn't want to live here.

16 - We are their friends.

17 - She doesn't like our garden.

18 - We don't know these people.

19 - Does your son love me?

20 - The Paxtons aren't in Paris.

1 - They've got our address. They haven't got our address.
2 - She works with you. Does she work with you?
3 - Are they with our sons? They aren't with our sons.
4 - She knows my name. Does she know my name?
5 - Do you have your new car? You don't have your new car.
6 - These people are your friends. These people aren't your friends.
7 - Does Betty work with us? Betty doesn't work with us.
8 - Have you got a new car? You haven't got a new car.
9 - Are the Wilsons in Glasgow? The Wilsons aren't in Glasgow.
10 - She knows I'm here. Does she know I'm here?
11 - Do we work with their son? We don't work with their son.
12 - Has he got our new address? He hasn't got our new address.
13 - Do the Spencers have this house? The Spencers don't have this house.
14 - Jenny is in the garage. Is Jenny in the garage?
15 - He wants to live here. Does he want to live here?
16 - Are we their friends? We aren't their friends.
17 - She likes our garden. Does she like our garden?
18 - We know these people. Do we know these people?
19 - Your son loves me. Your son doesn't love me.
20 - The Paxtons are in Paris. Are the Paxtons in Paris?

1 - She knows I live here.

2 - We aren't their cousins.

3 - You've got five children.

4 - Do they have Jack's address?

5 - Barbara doesn't live in Cork.

6 - Sarah is with her father.

7 - She doesn't work with us.

8 - Jim knows I live here.

9 - Their son isn't my friend.

10 - The Parkers have a new Rover.

11 - Does John work with you?

12 - Your sisters aren't with him.

13 - They don't work with Mark.

14 - Does she know my mother?

15 - They want to know you.

16 - These people are Jim's friends.

17 - Do you know this woman?

18 - Kim isn't with our daughter.

19 - Their parents work here.

20 - The children aren't in the garden.

1 - Does she know I live here? She doesn't know I live here.
2 - We are their cousins. Are we their cousins?
3 - Have you got five children? You haven't got five children.
4 - They have Jack's address. They don't have Jack's address.
5 - Barbara lives in Cork. Does Barbara live in Cork?
6 - Is Sarah with her father? Sarah isn't with her father.
7 - She works with us. Does she work with us?
8 - Does Jim know I live here? Jim doesn't know I live here.
9 - Their son is my friend. Is their son my friend?
10 - Do the Parkers have a new Rover? The Parkers don't have a new Rover.
11 - John works with you. John doesn't work with you.
12 - Your sisters are with him. Are your sisters with him?
13 - They work with Mark. Do they work with Mark?
14 - She knows my mother. She doesn't know my mother.
15 - They don't want to know you. Do they want to know you?
16 - Are these people Jim's friends? These people aren't Jim's friends.
17 – You know this woman. You don't know this woman.
18 - Kim is with our daughter. Is Kim with our daughter?
19 - Do their parents work here? Their parents don't work here.
20 - The children are in the garden. Are the children in the garden?

1 - You know these people.

2 - She works with my son.

3 - Are they your daughter's friends?

4 - She's got a new bedroom.

5 - They want to meet Bob.

6 - Sarah isn't their cousin.

7- They don't have their car.

8 - Does Jim work with you?

9 - They aren't with Pat's daughter.

10 - She's coming with her son.

11 - They want to meet me here.

12 - She works with my uncle.

13 - They know you are here.

14 - Have they got a new address?

15 - This new car is for Mike.

16 - You know I live here.

17 - Does he work with our friend?

18 - Jack's parents don't know you.

19 - Are these people French?

20 - She knows we are friends.

1 - Do you know these people? You don't know these people.
2 - Does she work with my son? She doesn't work with my son.
3 - They are your daughter's friends. They aren't your daughter's friends.
4 - Has she got a new bedroom? She hasn't got a new bedroom.
5 - Do they want to meet Bob. They don't want to meet Bob.
6 - Sarah is their cousin. Is Sarah their cousin?
7- They have their car. Do they have their car?
8 - Jim works with you. Jim doesn't work with you.
9 - They are with Pat's daughter. Are they with Pat's daughter?
10 - Is she coming with her son? She isn't coming with her son.
11 - Do they want to meet me here? They don't want to meet me here.
12 - Does she work with my uncle? She doesn't work with my uncle.
13 - Do they know you are here? They don't know you are here.
14 - They've got a new address. They haven't got a new address.
15 - Is this new car for Mike? This new car isn't for Mike.
16 - Do you know I live here? You don't know I live here.
17 - He works with our friend. He doesn't work with our friend.
18 - Jack's parents know you. Do Jack's parents know you?
19 - These people are French. These people aren't French.
20 - Does she know we are friends? She doesn't know we are friends.

1 - Are they with our cousins?

2 - She knows my sister's name.

3 - Have they got our new address?

4 - I want to meet Mr. Flint.

5 - These people work with Jo.

6 - Do they live in France?

7 - It's the Parkers' new garden.

8 - His sister likes my new friend.

9 - We've got a German car.

10 - They don't like to meet here.

11 - Their new house is in Rickie.

12 - The Wilsons have a new flat.

13 - Does he know that boy is French?

14 - Linda works with me in Cork.

15 - Your daughter knows this boy.

16 - The Spencers' garage is here.

17 - Has she got our new address?

18 - Malcolm has three cousins.

19 - Are they your son's new friends?

20 - She doesn't know we are here.

1 - They are with our cousins. They aren't with our cousins.
2 - Does she know my sister's name? She doesn't know my sister's name.
3 - They've got our new address. They haven't got our new address.
4 - Do I want to meet Mr. Flint? I don't want to meet Mr. Flint.
5 - Do these people work with Jo? These people don't work with Jo.
6 - They live in France. They don't live in France.
7 - Is it the Parkers' new garden? It isn't the Parkers' new garden.
8 - Does his sister like my new friend? His sister doesn't like my new friend.
9 - Have we got a German car? We haven't got a German car.
10 - They like to meet here. Do they like to meet here?
11 - Is their new house in Rickie? Their new house isn't in Rickie.
12 - Do the Wilsons have a new flat? The Wilsons don't have a new flat.
13 - He knows that boy is French. He doesn't know that boy is French.
14 - Does Linda work with me in Cork? Linda doesn't work with me in Cork.
15 - Does your daughter know this boy? Your daughter doesn't know this boy
16 - Is the Spencers' garage here? The Spencers' garage isn't here.
17 - She's got our new address. She hasn't got our new address.
18 - Does Malcolm have three cousins? Malcolm doesn't have three cousins.
19 - They are your son's new friends. They aren't your son's new friends.
20 - She knows we are here. Does she know we are here?

1 - She works with my cousin.

2 - He can come with his car.

3 - Do they like our new house?

4 - You mustn't work with Jane.

5 - Jim's got a new flat.

6 - Their children are in your car.

7 - Can they come with their car?

8 - Do you have a new address?

9 - She must live in London.

10 - She wants to meet them here.

11 - They are with Mary's son.

12 - You can have my bedroom.

13 - Our children like this old car.

14 - Does your sister work here?

15 - She must live with Jack's friend.

16 - They aren't your son's friends.

17 - She doesn't know your name.

18 - They can meet her in Cork.

19 - They meet him in Dublin.

20 - Can she work with Arthur?

1 - Does she work with my cousin? She doesn't work with my cousin.
2 - Can he come with his car? He can't come with his car.
3 - They like our new house. They don't like our new house.
4 - You must work with Jane. Must you work with Jane?
5 - Has Jim got a new flat? Jim hasn't got a new flat.
6 - Are their children in your car? Their children aren't in your car.
7 - They can come with their car. They can't come with their car.
8 - You have a new address. You don't have a new address.
9 - Must she live in London? She mustn't live in London.
10 - Does she want to meet them here? She doesn't want to meet them here.
11 - Are they with Mary's son? They aren't with Mary's son.
12 - Can you have my bedroom? You can't have my bedroom.
13 - Do our children like this old car? Our children don't like this old car.
14 - Your sister works here. Your sister doesn't work here.
15 - Must she live with Jack's friend? She mustn't live with Jack's friend.
16 - They are your son's friends. Are they your son's friends?
17 - She knows your name. Does she know your name?
18 - Can they meet her in Cork? They can't meet her in Cork.
19 - Do they meet him in Dublin? They don't meet him in Dublin.
20 - She can work with Arthur. She can't work with Arthur.

1 - They know Bill's address.

2 - Is that girl their daughter?

3 - She can't come with her son.

4 - They want to meet you here.

5 - We must work with his niece.

6 - Are your friends in the garage?

7 - She doesn't know our cousin.

8 - Can you come with Betty?

9 - Their mother must be in Leeds.

10 - Henry's got three nephews.

11 - He knows we want this car.

12 - Does she meet me in Paris?

13 - We mustn't meet her here.

14 - She knows my cousin's name.

15 - They can work with Peter.

16 - Peter has a new friend.

17 - We can't meet Linda here.

18 - She's got our new address.

19 - They don't know we live here.

20 - Your mother is in the bathroom.

1 - Do they know Bill's address? They don't know Bill's address.
2 - That girl is their daughter. That girl isn't their daughter.
3 - She can come with her son. Can she come with her son?
4 - Do they want to meet you here? They don't want to meet you here.
5 - Must we work with his niece? We mustn't work with his niece.
6 - Your friends are in the garage. Your friends aren't in the garage.
7 - She knows our cousin. Does she know our cousin.
8 - You can come with Betty. You can't come with Betty.
9 - Must their mother be in Leeds? Their mother mustn't be in Leeds.
10 - Has Henry got three nephews? Henry hasn't got three nephews.
11 - Does he know we want this car? He doesn't know we want this car.
12 - She meets me in Paris. She doesn't meet me in Paris.
13 - We must meet her here. Must we meet her here?
14 - Does she know my cousin's name? She doesn't know my cousin's name.
15 - Can they work with Peter? They can't work with Peter.
16 - Does Peter have a new friend? Peter doesn't have a new friend.
17 - We can meet Linda here. Can we meet Linda here?
18 - Has she got our new address? She hasn't got our new address.
19 - They know we live here. Do they know we live here?
20 - Is your mother in the bathroom? Your mother isn't in the bathroom.

1 - It's the Wilsons' new garden.

2 - They can come with my car.

3 - You've got my new room.

4 - Their daughter lives here.

5 - Her son isn't in our garden.

6 - Bob loves your friend.

7 - Must we come at 7 p.m?

8 - They are in Jack's room.

9 - Jill wants to meet you.

10 - These people are our friends.

11 - You can't go to Liverpool.

12 - Does her uncle work here?

13 - They must meet us here.

14 - Your son works with her.

15 - This is my friend's new car.

16 - They know we're here.

17 - Can you go to Oxford?

18 - He's got my new flat.

19 - The Palmers have three cars.

20 - It isn't their new house.

1 - Is it the Wilsons' new garden? It isn't the Wilsons' new garden.
2 - Can they come with my car? They can't come with my car.
3 - Have you got my new room? You haven't got my new room.
4 - Does their daughter live here? Their daughter doesn't live here.
5 - Her son is in our garden. Is her son in our garden?
6 - Does Bob love your friend? Bob doesn't love your friend.
7 - We must come at 7.p.m. We mustn't come at 7 p.m.
8 - Are they in Jack's room? They aren't in Jack's room.
9 - Does Jill want to meet you? Jill doesn't want to meet you.
10 - Are these people our friends? These people aren't our friends.
11 - You can go to Liverpool. Can you go to Liverpool?
12 - Her uncle works here. Her uncle doesn't work here.
13 - Must they meet us here? They mustn't meet us here.
14 - Does your son work with her? Your son doesn't work with her.
15 - Is this my friend's new car? This isn't my friend's new car.
16 - Do they know we're here? They don't know we're here.
17 - You can go to Oxford. You can't go to Oxford.
18 - Has he got my new flat? He hasn't got my new flat.
19 - Do the Palmers have three cars? The Palmers don't have three cars.
20 - It is their new house. Is it their new house?

1 - Does she live with George?

2 - Their new car is here.

3 - Henry can meet your son.

4 - She knows my address.

5 - His new flat isn't in London.

6 - They must be with Jo.

7 - Can Sarah live with you?

8 - This old woman is English.

9 - The Parkers know us.

10 - He knows I love you.

11 - Our children are with Tom.

12 - She can meet Kim here.

13 - That's Bob's new room.

14 - Does Mike want to come?

15 - She must work with Kevin.

16 - These cars are for us.

17 - Ted knows your son.

18 - She's got two sisters.

19 - Mark doesn't have his car.

20 - She is coming with him.

1 - She lives with George. She doesn't live with George.
2 - Is their new car here? Their new car isn't here.
3 - Can Henry meet your son? Henry can't meet your son.
4 - Does she know my address? She doesn't know my address.
5 - His new flat is in London. Is his new flat in London?
6 - Must they be with Jo? They mustn't be with Jo.
7 - Sarah can live with you. Sarah can't live with you.
8 - Is this old woman English? This old woman isn't English.
9 - Do the Parkers know us? The Parkers don't know us.
10 - Does he know I love you? He doesn't know I love you.
11 - Are our children with Tom? Our children aren't with Tom.
12 - Can she meet Kim here? She can't meet Kim here.
13 - Is that Bob's new room? That isn't Bob's new room.
14 - Mike wants to come. Mike doesn't want to come.
15 - Must she work with Kevin? She mustn't work with Kevin.
16 - Are these cars for us? These cars aren't for us.
17 - Does Ted know your son? Ted doesn't know your son.
18 - Has she got two sisters? She hasn't got two sisters.
19 - Mark has his car. Does Mark have his car?
20 - Is she coming with him? She isn't coming with him.

1 - Bill knows their name.

2 - They have to phone us

3 - Are Sally's friends in Cork?

4 - You don't like our flat.

5 - She knows they're here.

6 - Her uncle has his car.

7 - They don't want to meet you.

8 - Does Mike know her son?

9 - They aren't going to Galway.

10 - This woman is their aunt.

11 - Do they like our new garden?

12 - They've got a new house.

13 - She's going to meet them.

14 - Your friend's son isn't here.

15 - Her nephew doesn't live in Italy.

16 - Do they know we prefer you?

17 - Jill's daughter isn't in Leeds.

18 - Our friend is coming at 7.

19 - He doesn't want to meet her.

20 - These people aren't her friends.

1 - Does Bill know their name? Bill doesn't know their name.
2 - Do they have to phone us? They don't have to phone us.
3 - Sally's friends are in Cork. Sally's friends aren't in Cork.
4 - You like our flat. Do you like our flat?
5 - Does she know they're here? She doesn't know they're here.
6 - Does her uncle have his car? Her uncle doesn't have his car.
7 - They want to meet you. Do they want to meet you?
8 - Mike knows her son. Mike doesn't know her son.
9 - They are going to Galway. Are they going to Galway?
10 - Is this woman their aunt? This woman isn't their aunt.
11 - They like our new garden. They don't like our new garden.
12 - Have they got a new house? They haven't got a new house.
13 - Is she going to meet them? She isn't going to meet them.
14 - Your friend's son is here. Is your friend's son here?
15 - Her nephew lives in Italy. Does her nephew live in Italy?
16 - They know we prefer you. They don't know we prefer you.
17 - Jill's daughter is in Leeds. Is Jill's daughter in Leeds?
18 - Is our friend coming at 7? Our friend isn't coming at 7.
19 - He wants to meet her. Does he want to meet her?
20 - These people are her friends. Are these people her friends?

1 - That's Jack's new flat.

2 - Do they work with you?

3 - Paula's son doesn't work with her.

4 - Your cousin isn't coming.

5 - They have to come at 5.

6 - She must work with us.

7 - This old house isn't for them.

8 - Do I know her new friend?

9 - That's Malcolm's new car.

10 - Her mother isn't in the kitchen.

11 - Luke doesn't want to work here.

12 - Are these people Jo's friends?

13 - The Wilsons like that car.

14 - She doesn't live with Bill Fox.

15 - The Turners aren't her friends.

16 - Our new car is in the garage.

17 - She doesn't love Edgar's nephew.

18 - Barbara's niece isn't in Paris.

19 - They can't come with Jane.

20 - Must Henry go to London?

1 - Is that Jack's new flat? That isn't Jack's new flat.
2 - They work with you. They don't work with you.
3 - Paula's son works with her. Does Paula's son work with her?
4 - Your cousin is coming. Is your cousin coming?
5 - Do they have to come at 5? They don't have to come at 5.
6 - Must she work with us? She mustn't work with us.
7 - This old house is for them. Is this old house for them?
8 - I know her new friend. I don't know her new friend.
9 - Is that Malcolm's new car? That isn't Malcolm's new car.
10 - Her mother is in the kitchen. Is her mother in the kitchen?
11 - Luke wants to work here. Does Luke want to work here?
12 - These people are Jo's friends. These people aren't Jo's friends.
13 - Do the Wilsons like that car? The Wilsons don't like that car.
14 - She lives with Bill Fox. Does she live with Bill Fox?
15 - The Turners are her friends. Are the Turners her friends?
16 - Is our new car in the garage? Our new car isn't in the garage.
17 - She loves Edgar's nephew. Does she love Edgar's nephew?
18 - Barbara's niece is in Paris. Is Barbara's niece in Paris?
19 - They can come with Jane. Can they come with Jane?
20 - Henry must go to London. Henry mustn't go to London.

Résumé Grammatical Etape 0/5

Questions en WH :

Pour poser une question en « qui, où, quand, comment, pourquoi, etc. » il suffit d'ajouter le pronom interrogatif voulu devant la forme interrogative :

Where does he work? = **Où** travaille-t-il ?
Why are you here? = **Pourquoi** êtes-vous ici ?

Question = **WH + AUX + SUJET + VERBE** (+ Complément le cas échéant)
          Ou **WH + BE + SUJET +…** (pour le cas du verbe Etre)

Les principaux pronoms interrogatifs (WH) sont :

Qui	**Who**
Où	**Where**
Quand	**When**
Comment	**How**
Pourquoi	**Why**
Combien	**How many** (plur.) **How much** (sing.)
Que/ Qu'est-ce que	**What**
Quel(le)(s) / lequel, etc.	**Which** (particulier) **What** (général)
Quelle heure	**What time**
Quelle distance	**How far**
Quelle fréquence :	**How often**

Remarque 1 : Pas de construction interrogative possible quand le WH représente le sujet de la phrase :

Who do you prefer? = Qui préférez-vous ? (Who = Complément)
Who phones you? = Qui vous téléphone ? (Who = Sujet) (pas d'interrogatif)

Remarque 2 : Quand le WH questionne un complément indirect, c'est-à-dire séparé du verbe par un mot de liaison, ce dernier reste à la toute fin de la question (à l'inverse du français où il débute la question) :

Avec qui travailles-tu ? = Who do you work **with**?
D'où est votre amie ? = Where is your friend **from**?

Remarque 3 : Pour interroger le possesseur, on utilise « Whose » signifiant « à qui » ou « de qui » au sens possessif des termes.

A qui est ce livre ? = C'est le livre de qui ? = **Whose** book is it ?

Noter que « whose », comme « which », et « how much » ou « how many », sont toujours immédiatement accompagnés du mot qu'ils concernent.

How many **children** do you have ? = Combien d'enfants as-tu ?
Which **car** do you prefer? = Quelle voiture préférez-vous ?

En utilisant ces données, questionner la partie soulignée des phrases suivantes, puis corriger à la fin de chaque page.

1 - Mark is <u>Barbara's brother</u>.

2 - She works <u>in Liverpool</u>.

3 - He wants to <u>work here</u>.

4 - He prefers to live <u>in France</u>.

5 - She prefers <u>this</u> house?

6 - They come <u>at 4 p.m</u>.

7 - The children are <u>in the kitchen</u>.

8 – He comes <u>by car</u>.

9 - He wants <u>three</u> books.

10 - Your son lives with <u>Kim</u>.

11 - He likes to work in <u>this room</u>.

12 - She prefers to come <u>at 6</u>.

13 - <u>Jennifer</u> knows the Foxes' address.

14 - The Wilsons have <u>three</u> cars.

15 - You want to work <u>in Paris</u>.

16 - They are here <u>because they want to meet you</u>.

17 - He prefers to work with <u>Alison</u>.

18 - The Paxtons live <u>in Scotland</u>.

19 - They prefer to come <u>by train</u>.

20 - They've got <u>two</u> children.

1 - Who is Mark?

2 - Where does she work?

3 - What does he want to do?

4 - Where does he prefer to live?

5 - Which house does she prefer?

6 - What time do they come?

7 - Where are the children?

8 – How does he come?

9 - How many books does he want?

10 - Who does your son live with?

11 - Where does he like to work?

12 - What time does she prefer to come?

13 - Who knows the Foxes' address?

14 - How many cars do the Wilsons have?

15 - Where do you want to work?

16 - Why are they here?

17 - Who does he prefer to work with?

18 - Where do the Paxtons live?

19 - How do they prefer to come?

20 - How many children have they got?

1 - This book is for <u>William</u>.

2 - She's here <u>because she's my friend</u>.

3 - They know <u>Mr Miller's son</u>.

4 - Mr Brown works <u>in Liverpool</u>.

5 - Henry's children are <u>in the garage</u>.

6 - He prefers her <u>because she's English</u>.

7 - Their daughter is <u>in Wendy's room</u>.

8 - He prefers <u>the blue</u> car.

9 - They want to go <u>to Banbury</u>.

10 - She lives with <u>Jane's son</u>.

11 - These people are <u>our daughter's friends</u>.

12 - They want to come <u>at 10 a.m.</u>

13 - Jim prefers <u>to work</u> today.

14 - She meets your friend <u>in London</u>.

15 - He knows you <u>because you work here</u>.

16 - Their new car is <u>in our garage</u>.

17 - She's got a flat <u>in Leeds</u>.

18 - They have <u>three</u> friends in America.

19 - Malcolm is <u>thirty years</u> old.

20 - This old car is for <u>Betty's brother</u>.

1 - Who is this book for?

2 - Why is she here?

3 - Who do they know?

4 - Where does Mr. Brown work?

5 - Where are Henry's children?

6 - Why does he prefer her?

7 - Where is their daughter?

8 - Which car does he prefer?

9 - Where do they want to go (to)?

10 - Who does she live with?

11 - Who are these people?

12 - What time do they want to come?

13 - What does Jim prefer to do today?

14 - Where does she meet your friend?

15 - How does he know you?

16 - Where is their new car?

17 - Where has she got a flat?

18 - How many friends do they have in America?

19 - How old is Malcolm?

20 - Who is this old car for?

1 - The Wilsons come <u>at 5.30</u>.

2 - He prefers to play with <u>Jim</u>?

3 - Her daughter works <u>in Liverpool</u>.

4 - They prefer <u>the red</u> car.

5 - He's got <u>a Rover</u>.

6 - They prefer to come <u>at 7 p.m</u>.

7 - Your son lives <u>in Ireland</u>.

8 – He comes here <u>by bus</u>.

9 - They prefer to phone <u>Bernie</u>.

10 - She works with <u>Bob's sister</u>.

11 - The Wilsons have <u>3</u> cats.

12 - Their son is with <u>his friends</u>.

13 - Sue wants to <u>go to France</u>.

14 - Jo's parents are <u>at the restaurant</u>.

15 - She prefers to meet him <u>in London</u>.

16 - He works here <u>because he's French</u>.

17 - Bill prefers <u>William</u>'s car.

18 - They've got <u>two</u> garages.

19 - She knows him <u>because he works with me</u>.

20 - <u>Mr Krammer</u> works with Marian.

1 - What time do the Wilsons come?
2 - Who does he prefer to play with?
3 - Where does her daughter work?
4 - Which car do they prefer?
5 - What car has he got?
6 - What time do they prefer to come?
7 - Where does your son live?
8 - How does he come here?
9 - Who do they prefer to phone?
10 - Who does she work with?
11 - How many cats do the Wilsons have?
12 - Who is their son with?
13 - What does Sue want to do?
14 - Where are Jo's parents?
15 - Where does she prefer to meet him?
16 - Why does he work here?
17 - Whose car does Bill prefer?
18 - How many garages have they got?
19 - How does she know him?
20 - Who works with Marian?

1 - She meets him in our flat.

2 - Steve wants to work with us.

3 - They prefer to live in Paris.

4 - Barbara's got a new address.

5 - Our cousins are at the restaurant.

6 - They meet on Monday evenings.

7 - Sarah prefers the Spencers' house.

8 - The black car is for Mr. Fox.

9 - This bedroom is for your friends.

10 - William's new Ford is blue.

11 - Their father is 65 years old.

12 - They go to Leeds every morning.

13 - Sandy prefers to meet the Nortons' daughter.

14 – She prefers to work in her room.

15 - Your son's car is in our garage.

16 - Sharon works with a Frenchman.

17 - The yellow bedroom is for Jackie.

18 - They prefer Christopher's car.

19 - His mother comes at 5.30.

20 - Their friends live in Manchester.

1 - Where does she meet him?

2 - Who does Steve want to work with?

3 - Where do they prefer to live?

4 - Who's got a new address?

5 - Where are our cousins?

6 - When do they meet?

7 - Whose house does Sarah prefer?

8 - Which car is for Mr. Fox?

9 - Who is this bedroom for?

10 - What colour is William's new Ford?

11 - How old is their father?

12 - When (How often) do they go to Leeds?

13 – Who does Sandy prefer to meet?

14 – What does she prefer to do in her room?

15 - Where is your son's car?

16 - Who does Sharon work with?

17 - Which bedroom is for Jackie?

18 - Whose car do they prefer?

19 - What time does his mother come?

20 - Where do their friends live?

1 - They have <u>three</u> garages.

2 - They can work <u>in the living-room</u>.

3 - Sarah knows <u>Steve's address</u>.

4 - They want to meet us <u>here</u>.

5 - They must come <u>on Monday</u>.

6 - He is here <u>because he loves you</u>.

7 - She wants to be <u>in the garden</u>.

8 - This young boy is <u>Bob's son</u>.

9 - She's got <u>two</u> brothers.

10 - These people are <u>Jo</u>'s friends.

11 – They prefer to come <u>by train</u>.

12 - Jack prefers <u>the green</u> car.

13 - The Watsons have <u>an Audi</u>.

14 - Her sister lives <u>in Brighton</u>.

15 - Peter <u>works</u> in Manchester.

16 - Jenny must phone <u>her uncle</u>.

17 - Henry's aunt is from <u>leeds</u>.

18 - This new car is for <u>Walter</u>.

19 - She can come <u>at 3.p.m</u>.

20 - They meet their friends <u>in Cork</u>.

1 - How many garages do they have?

2 - Where can they work?

3 - What does Sarah know?

4 - Where do they want to meet us?

5 - When must they come?

6 - Why is he here?

7 - Where does she want to be?

8 - Who is this young boy?

9 - How many brothers has she got?

10 - Whose friends are these people?

11 – How do they prefer to come?

12 - Which car does Jack prefer?

13 - What car do the Watsons have?

14 - Where does her sister live?

15 - What does Peter do in Manchester?

16 - Who must Jenny phone?

17 - Where is Henry's aunt from?

18 - Who is this new car for?

19 - What time can she come?

20 - Where do they meet their friends?

1 - She prefers Johanna's flat.
2 - The Wallsons live in Pembroke.
3 - Henry's new car is green.
4 - Sharon works with Mr. Flint.
5 – He comes here when he wants to meet Jo.
6 - Mr. Walker prefers to go to Hull at 8 p.m.
7 - The Browns come on Thursdays.
8 - They want to meet the Wilkinsons.
9 - Your son prefers the black car.
10 - Fiona prefers to meet us here.
11 - He knows her name because she's his cousin.
12 - The Jones have 4 children.
13 - She's got my sister's address.
14 - Their friends work in Watford.
15 - We're here because Liz wants to meet Mr. Fox.
16 - Jo's father prefers to go to London.
17 - They can come at 9 a.m.
18 - Your brother's got 2 cars.
19 - They want to work in the living-room.
20 - She prefers to come with her cousin.

1 - Whose flat does she prefer?

2 - Where do the Wallsons live?

3 - What colour is Henry's new car?

4 - Who does Sharon work with?

5 - When does he come here?

6 - What time does Mr. Walker prefer to go to Hull?

7 - When do the Browns come?

8 - Who do they want to meet?

9 - Which car does your son prefer.

10 - Where does Fiona prefer to meet us?

11 - How does he know her name?

12 - How many children do the Jones have?

13 - Whose address has she got?

14 - What do their friends do in Watford?

15 - Why are we here?

16 - What does Jo's father prefer to do?

17 - What time can they come?

18 - How many cars has your brother got?

19 - Where do they want to work?

20 - Who does she prefer to come with?

1 - These books are for <u>our nephews</u>.

2 - She prefers to play with <u>Kim</u>.

3 - Stan's daughter loves <u>Mark</u>.

4 - Bernie wants to <u>meet the Grants</u>.

5 - These boys are <u>my brother's friends</u>.

6 - Sarah's new address is <u>in Manchester</u>.

7 - Linda is here <u>because she knows Mr. Fox</u>.

8 - They've got <u>three</u> cousins in Germany.

9 - William's friends live <u>in Pembroke</u>.

10 - <u>Mr. Smith</u> prefers to be with us.

11 - Their new German car is <u>grey</u>.

12 - The children <u>play</u> in their room.

13 - Your son knows <u>our French friends</u>.

14 - That red car is for <u>your daughter</u>.

15 - Jim wants to meet Sally <u>in Leeds</u>.

16 - This car is <u>your uncle</u>'s.

17 - They prefer to come here <u>by car</u>.

18 - Lewis works with <u>Jim's nephew</u>.

19 - <u>Johanna</u> lives with Mr. Flag.

20 - She wants to <u>meet our cousin Henry</u>.

1 - Who are these books for?

2 - Who does she prefer to play with?

3 - Who does Stan's daughter love?

4 - What does Bernie want to do?

5 - Who are these boys?

6 - Where is Sarah's new address?

7 - Why is Linda here?

8 - How many cousins have they got in Germany?

9 - Where do William's friends live?

10 - Who prefers to be with us?

11 - What colour is their new German car?

12 - What do the children do in their room?

13 - Who does your son know?

14 - Who is that red car for?

15 - Where does Jim want to meet Sally?

16 - Whose car is this?

17 - How do they prefer to come here?

18 - Who does Lewis work with?

19 - Who lives with Mr. Flag?

20 - What does she want to do?

1 - The Paxtons have <u>2</u> houses.

2 - Sandy prefers to come <u>at 4.30 p.m.</u>

3 - These new books are for <u>your children</u>.

4 - She can work with <u>Mr. Wilson's nephew</u>.

5 - We must be <u>in London</u> at 5 a.m.

6 - They are here <u>because they know Willie</u>.

7 - Her uncle wants to <u>meet Jackie Marlow</u>.

8 - Tom prefers <u>his cousin</u>'s car.

9 - Betty likes to work <u>in her sister's room</u>.

10 - He's got <u>2</u> brothers and <u>3</u> sisters.

11 - They prefer to go to Cork <u>on Wednesday</u>.

12 - <u>Their children</u> are in your aunt's garage.

13 - Sharon works with <u>our nephew's friend</u>.

14 - Bill can go to Amersham <u>by train</u>.

15 - Mr Flint's niece lives <u>in Liverpool</u>.

16 - Johnny prefers <u>the green</u> bedroom.

17 - The Parkers prefer to meet you <u>here</u>.

18 - Their daughter comes <u>on Fridays</u>.

19 - She works here <u>because she's their cousin</u>.

20 - Their son can meet me <u>in Windsor</u>.

1 - How many houses do the Paxtons have?

2 - What time does Sandy prefer to come?

3 - Who are these new books for?

4 - Who can she work with?

5 - Where must we be at 5.a.m.?

6 - Why are they here?

7 - What does her uncle want to do?

8 - Whose car does Tom prefer?

9 - Where does Betty like to work?

10 - How many brothers and sisters has he got?

11 - When do they prefer to go to Cork?

12 - Who is in your aunt's garage?

13 - Who does Sharon work with?

14 - How can Bill go to Amersham?

15 - Where does Mr Flint's niece live?

16 - Which bedroom does Johnny prefer?

17 - Where do the Parkers prefer to meet you?

18 - When does their daughter come?

19 - Why does she work here?

20 - Where can their son meet me?

1 - Mike's parents are <u>in the kitchen</u>.

2 - They come here <u>every day</u>.

3 - She must be in Leeds <u>at 5 o'clock</u>.

4 - This is <u>Christopher</u>'s car.

5 - He's here to <u>meet Mr Spencer</u>.

6 - Their cousins live <u>in Madrid</u>.

7 - <u>Sandra</u> wants to meet us in Hull.

8 - They prefer to work with <u>Harry</u>.

9 - The Millers have <u>2</u> children.

10 - This new American car is for <u>Malcolm</u>.

11 - You work with <u>Professor Smith</u>.

12 - Their friends prefer <u>this</u> car.

13 - She is here <u>to meet Edgar's uncle</u>.

14 - They want to have <u>Fiona</u>'s address.

15 - We must <u>meet the Stones</u> on Tuesday.

16 - Tommy's new address is <u>in Scotland</u>.

17 - This is <u>Wendy Marlow</u>'s house.

18 - She knows him <u>because he works here</u>.

19 - They can meet <u>our friends</u> in Paris.

20 - Maggie's car is <u>in her parents' garage</u>.

1 - Where are Mike's parents?

2 - How often do they come here?

3 - What time must she be in Leeds?

4 - Whose car is this?

5 - Why is he here? (What is he here for?)

6 - Where do their cousins live?

7 - Who wants to meet us in Hull?

8 - Who do they prefer to work with?

9 - How many children do the Millers have?

10 - Who is this new American car for?

11 - Who do you work with?

12 - Which car do their friends prefer?

13 - What is she here for? (Why is she here?)

14 - Whose address do they want to have.

15 - What must we do on Tuesday?

16 - Where is Tommy's new address?

17 - Whose house is this?

18 - How does she know him?

19 - Who can they meet in Paris?

20 - Where is Maggie's car?

1 - Sue wants to know <u>their new address</u>.

2 - They must <u>phone us</u> at 5 p.m.

3 - Linda can meet Mrs Fox <u>at the restaurant</u>.

4 - This address is for <u>your French friends</u>.

5 - Their children are <u>in our living-room</u>.

6 - <u>Her brother</u> works with my daughter.

7 - She prefers to meet <u>our new friends</u>.

8 - They've got <u>three</u> nephews.

9 - She knows him <u>because he's English</u>.

10 - This is <u>the Nortons</u>' house.

11 - They come here <u>to meet Paul</u>.

12 - These old books are for <u>our father</u>.

13 - She prefers to be <u>in the kitchen</u>.

14 - He must phone his parents <u>on Sunday</u>.

15 - They can meet <u>our uncle</u> in this room.

16 - Fred knows I'm French <u>because he works here</u>.

17 – He prefers <u>the Millers</u>' car.

18 - The Nortons are <u>Mr Wilkinson</u>'s friends.

19 - We've got <u>fifteen</u> cousins in Europe.

20 - They prefer to work with <u>George</u>.

1 - What does Sue want to know?

2 - What must they do at 5 p.m.?

3 - Where can Linda meet Mrs Fox?

4 - Who is this address for?

5 - Where are their children?

6 - Who works with my daughter?

7 - Who does she prefer to meet?

8 - How many nephews have they got?

9 - How does she know him?

10 - Whose house is this?

11 - What do they come here for? (Why do they come here?)

12 - Who are these old books for?

13 - Where does she prefer to be?

14 - When (What day) must he phone his parents?

15 - Who can they meet in this room?

16 - How does Fred know I'm French?

17 - Whose car does he prefer?

18 - Whose friends are the Nortons?

19 - How many cousins have we got in Europe?

20 - Who do they prefer to work with?

1 - The Palmers live in Pembroke.

2 - They've got 3 friends in Italy.

3 - This bedroom is for your cousin.

4 - She can come here at 6.30.

5 - Audrey must phone her uncle this morning.

6 – They go to Dublin by plane.

7 - Sarah wants to work with my nephew.

8 - Patrick works with our father.

9 - Their new car is in William's garage.

10 - She knows Bob because he works here.

11 - Their friends prefer Betty's room.

12 - We must meet the Nortons in Paris.

13 - Henry has to phone his sister at 3 p.m.

14 - Mark's cousins meet Sally on Fridays.

15 - This address is for your mother's friend.

16 - They want to meet our parents here.

17 - She prefers to work in our restaurant.

18 - Our sister's friend is from Manchester.

19 - This is Professor Wilkinson's bedroom.

20 - They meet here because Alice works here.

1 - Where do the Palmers live?

2 - How many friends have they got in Italy?

3 - Who is this bedroom for?

4 - What time can she come here?

5 - Who must Audrey phone this morning?

6 - How do they go to Dublin?

7 - Who wants to work with my nephew?

8 - Who does Patrick work with?

9 - Where is their new car?

10 - How does she know Bob?

11 - Whose room do their friends prefer?

12 - What must we do in Paris?

13 - What time does Henry have to phone his sister?

14 - When do Mark's cousins meet Sally?

15 - Who is this address for?

16 - What do they want to do here?

17 - Where does she prefer to work?

18 - Where is our sister's friend from?

19 - Whose bedroom is this?

20 - Why do they meet here?

1 - These people are <u>my cousins' friends</u>.

2 - Wendy's son works with <u>my nephew</u>.

3 - They work in <u>Liverpool</u>.

4 - We can meet the Wilsons <u>in your house</u>.

5 - He is here <u>to meet our French friends</u>.

6 - My sister prefers <u>Christopher</u>'s car.

7 - This new flat is for <u>our nephew</u>.

8 - You want to meet <u>my mother's friend</u>.

9 – They prefer to go <u>to Blackpool</u>.

10 - She knows my name <u>because you are friends</u>.

11 - Their daughter <u>lives and works</u> in Paris.

12 - Her brother prefers to play <u>in his room</u>.

13 - Sharon wants to meet <u>our friends</u> here.

14 - This new book is for <u>Barbara's aunt</u>.

15 - They must come with <u>their son</u>.

16 - We can phone the Wilsons <u>at 9 p.m</u>.

17 - They've got <u>three</u> garages in London.

18 - The Foxes have <u>a new flat</u> in Leeds?

19 - He prefers to <u>play tennis</u> with us.

20 – Sharon wants <u>to meet our parents</u>.

1 - Who are these people?
2 - Who does Wendy's son work with?
3 - Where do they work?
4 - Where can we meet the Wilsons?
5 - What is he here for? (Why is he here?)
6 - Whose car does my sister prefer?
7 - Who is this new flat for?
8 - Who do you want to meet?
9 - Where do they prefer to go (to)?
10 - How does she know my name?
11 - What does their daughter do in Paris?
12 - Where does her brother prefer to play?
13 - Who does Sharon want to meet here?
14 - Who is this new book for?
15 - Who must they come with?
16 - What time can we phone the Wilsons?
17 - How many garages have they got in London?
18 - What do the Foxes have in Leeds?
19 - What does he prefer to do with us?
20 - What does Sharon want to do?

VOCABULAIRE

à + ville / pays :	**in** (à Paris = in Paris)
à + lieu précis :	**at** (à la gare = at the station)
à + direction :	**to** (aller à = to go to ; venir à = to come to…)
adresse :	address
aimer :	to like / to love
aller (à / en):	**to go** (to) (+ lieu)
américain :	American
Amérique :	America
ami(e) :	friend
anglais(e) :	English
Angleterre :	England
appartement :	**flat**
à qui (possessif):	**whose** (+ N) (A qui est cette voiture ? Whose car is this?)
avec :	with
avoir :	to have (he/she/it **has**)
chambre :	**bedroom** (room si possesseur précisé : Jack's room)
ce / cet, cette :	this / that
ces :	these
combien :	how many (+ pluriel); how much (+ singulier)
comment :	**how** (quel âge = how old / quelle distance = how far)
connaître :	to know
couleur :	colour (De quelle couleur = What colour)
cousin(e) :	cousin
cuisine (pièce) :	kitchen
dans :	in
devoir :	**must** (+ infinitif sans to) (remplace "do" pour FI/FN)
en (+ pays)	**in** (en France = in France)
enfant :	child ; pluriel : **children**
et :	and
être :	**to be** : I **am**, you **are**, he/she/it **is**, we **are,** you **are**; they **are**.
faire :	to do (troisième personne he/she/it **does**)
femme :	woman ; pluriel : **women**
fille :	**girl / daughter**. (Une fille = A girl. Ma fille = My daughter)
fils :	son

français :	French
France :	France
frère :	brother
garage :	garage
garçon :	boy
gens :	people
habiter :	to live
heure :	time (Quelle heure…= What time) (« hour » pour une durée)
homme :	man ; pluriel : **men**
ici :	here
jardin :	garden
jeune :	young
la (+ nom) :	the
le (+ nom) :	the
les (+ nom) :	the
livre :	book
maison :	house
mère :	mother
neveu :	nephew
nièce :	niece
nom :	name
nouveau :	new
nouvelle :	new
oncle :	uncle
où :	where
parce que :	because
parents :	parents
père :	father
pièce :	room
pour :	**for** (+ nom ou pronom) ; **to** (+ verbe)
pourquoi :	why
pour quoi faire:	what…..**for** ?
pouvoir :	**can** (+ infinitif sans to) (remplace « do » pour FI/FN)
préférer :	to prefer
que, qu' :	what
quel(le), quels :	what (contexte général) ; **which** (contexte spécifique : lequel)
quand :	when ; fréquence : **how often**
qui :	who
rencontrer :	to meet
restaurant :	restaurant
salle de bain :	bathroom

salon :	living-room
savoir (que) :	to know
soeur :	sister
tante :	aunt
travailller :	to work
un / une :	a (+ mot commençant par une consonne),
un /une :	an (+ mot commençant par une voyelle)
venir :	**to come** to (à) / from (de)
vieux/vieil(le):	old
vivre :	to live
voiture :	car
vouloir :	to want

Pronoms sujets

je	I
tu	you
il / elle	**he** (m) **she** (f) **it** (n)
nous	we
vous	you
ils / elles	they

Pronoms compléments

me, moi, m'	me
te, toi, t'	you
le, la, lui, elle,	**him** (m) **her** (f) **it** (n)
nous	us
vous	you
les, eux, leur	them

Adjectifs possessifs

mon, ma, mes	my
ton, ta, tes	your
son, sa, ses	**his** (à lui), **her** (à elle), **its** (objet)
notre, nos	our
votre, vos	your
leur(s) (+nom)	their

Prononciation simplifiée
(Prononcer à la française, en accentuant la syllabe soulignée le cas échéant)

à	in	inn'
à	at	att'
à	to	tou
adresse	address	eu-dresse (US ai dreuss)
aimer	to like	tou laïc
aimer	to love	tou lav'
aller	to go	tou gueu-o
américain	American	eumairikeun
Amérique	America	eumairikeu
Ami(e)	friend	frènn'd
Anglais(se)	English	inn'gliche
Angleterre	England	ingleund
Appartement	flat	flat (US **apartment** eupartmeunt)
à qui	whose	hhouze
avec	with	ouiv'
avoir	to have	tou hèv'
chambre	bedroom	bèd-roum
ce, cet, cette	this	dix (disse)
ce, cet cette	that	date
ces	these	dise (dize)
combien	how many	ha-o maini
combien	how much	ha-o match
comment	how	ha-o
connaître	to know	tou neu-ou
couleur	colour	kalor
cousin	cousin	kazeun
cuisine	kitchen	kitch'n
dans	in	inn'
devoir	must	mast'
enfant	child	tcha-ïl-de
enfants	children	tchildreunn
et	and	aenn
être	to be	tou bi-i
faire	to do	tou dou-ou
fait (il/elle)	does	daz
femme	woman	woumeun'
femmes	women	ouimène
fille	girl	gueurle

fille	daughter	dô-ôteur
fils	son	sonne
français(e)	French	frênntch
France	France	frènnce
frère	brother	braveur
garage	garage	garidj (US : gueurââge)
garcon	boy	boï-eu
gens	people	pi-i-pol
habiter	to live	tou liv'
heure	time	ta-ï-m'
homme	man	manne
hommes	men	mènne
ici	here	hi-eu
jardin	garden	gârdeun
jeune	young	yang
le, la, les	the	de
livre	book	bouc
maison	house	ha-ousse
mère	mother	maveur
neveu	nephew	naifiou
nièce	niece	ni-isse
nom	name	nê-imm'
nouveau (velle)	new	niou
oncle	uncle	un-col
où	where	hhouère
parce que	because	bikoz
parents	parents	paireunts
père	father	faveur
pièce	room	rou-oum
pour	for	for
pourquoi	why	hhouaille
pouvoir	can	kènn
pouvoir (nég)	can't	quante
préférer	to prefer	tou preufeur
que, quoi quel	what	hhouott'
qu'est-ce que	what	hhouott'
quel, lequel	which	hhouitche
quand	when	hhouènn'
quand (fréquence)	how often	hao-ofeunn'
qui	who	hhhouou
rencontrer	to meet	tou mii-ite

restaurant	restaurant	<u>rest</u>-reunt'	
salle de bain	bathroom	b<u>â</u>f-roum'	
séjour, salon	living-room	<u>li</u>vinne-roum'	
savoir (que)	to know	tou <u>neu</u>-ou	
sœur	sister	<u>sis</u>teur	
tante	aunt	ante	
travailler	to work	tou ou<u>eu</u>rk	
un(e)	a	eu	
un(e)	an	ann'	
venir	to come	tou kamm'	
vieux, vieil(le)	old	<u>eu</u>-ould	
vivre	to live	tou liv'	
voiture	car	câ-ââ	
vouloir	to want	tou ou<u>an</u>te	

<u>pronoms sujets :</u>	je	I	aïe
	tu	you	iou
	il	he	hhi
	elle	she	shi
	il/elle (objet)	it	itt
	nous	we	oui
	vous	you	iou
	ils/elles	they	deï
<u>pronoms compléments :</u>	me, moi	me	mii
	te, toi	you	iou
	le, lui (m)	him	hhimm
	la, lui (f)	her	hheure
	le, la, (objet)	it	itt
	nous	us	asse
	vous	you	iou
	les, leur (+V)	eux them	dèmm
<u>Adjectifs possessifs :</u>	mon, ma mes	my	maille
	ton, ta, tes	your	<u>iou</u>re
	son, sa, ses (m)	his	hhiz
	son, sa, ses (f)	her	hheur
	son, sa ses, (n)	its	itss
	notre	our	<u>a</u>-ou-eu
	votre	your	<u>iou</u>re
	leur (+nom)	their	dê-eu

What next ?

Les structures grammaticales que vous venez d'installer très solidement grâce aux cinq paliers de ce Niveau 0 de Saintélangues constituent déjà une base solide pour vous exprimer en toute situation présente usuelle, à la façon d'une trousse de survie touristique que vous pouvez déjà enrichir de n'importe quel vocabulaire complémentaire.

Vous voilà désormais bien préparé(e) pour réussir sans aucun risque les Niveaux 1A/1B/1C de Saintélangues si vous étiez au départ re-débutant(e), tandis qu'un(e) débutant(e) intégral(e) aura nettement intérêt à passer par les niveaux 0A/0B/0C.

....See you soon with Saintélangues!

B.G

Si vous avez apprécié...

...merci de vous connecter quelques instants sur Amazon.fr pour donner votre avis sur cet ouvrage et en recommander la lecture le cas échéant.

Votre avis est en effet essentiel, non seulement pour l'auteur et compositeur amateur que je suis, mais plus encore pour les nombreuses personnes surfant sur Internet en quête de conseils authentiques pour faire leur choix, sans compter que le soutien et les commentaires de mes lecteurs ou interprètes me sont tout aussi précieux que l'indispensable information des médias.

Dans l'attente du plaisir de vous lire en retour...

Bernard GARDE

Autres ouvrages disponibles du même auteur :

Âpre Miel
La conscience est amère, mais l'humour est sucré. (Ana)
Disponible sur Amazon.fr

Rapport Saintélangues
De l'échec à la réussite en Anglais. (Essai)
Disponible sur Amazon.fr

Corbeau Noir et Faisan Doré
(Roman policier)
Disponible sur Amazon.fr

English Dialogues 1 & 2
(52 dialogues en anglais et 1.100 questions de compréhension ou d'improvisation, avec traduction indicative intégrale). (2 volumes)
Disponible sur Amazon.fr

Le Ménestrin
(20 partitions pour flûte(s) à bec et dulcimer).
Disponible sur Amazon.fr

Cantate au Clair de Lune
(Pour voix ou instrument solo sur l'adagio de la Sonate au Clair de Lune de L.V. Beethoven).
Disponible sur Amazon.fr

Mélodithèque (Volumes 1 à 6)
(210 partitions pour guitare, guitare et flûte à bec, duos, trios et quatuors de flûtes à bec + enregistrements numériques).
Disponibles sur Free-scores.fr

Arrangements Musicaux
(The rose of Allendale, Amazing Grace, The Wild Rover, Scarborough Fair, Greensleeves, Canon de Pachelbel... + enregistrements numériques).
Disponibles sur Free-scores.fr

Saintélangues 0A / 0B / 0C
(Méthode autonome d'apprentissage pour re-débutant souhaitant consolider les acquis de Saintélangues niv.0 et enrichir son vocabulaire avant d'accéder au niveau 1). Trois volumes. Disponible sur Amazon.fr

Saintélangues 1A / 1B / 1C
(Méthode autonome d'apprentissage accéléré pour lycéens, étudiants et adultes. Niveau consolidation sur trois volumes). Disponible sur Amazon.fr

Saintélangues 2A / 2B / 2C
(Méthode autonome d'apprentissage accéléré pour lycéens, étudiants et adultes. Niveau perfectionnement sur trois volumes). Disponible sur Amazon.fr

Saintélangues 3A / 3B
(Méthode autonome de perfectionnement idiomatique pour étudiants et adultes. Niveau prépas, grandes écoles ou anglais spécialiste, sur deux volumes). Disponible sur Amazon.fr

www.ingramcontent.com/pod-product-compliance
Lightning Source LLC
Chambersburg PA
CBHW071509040426
42444CB00008B/1555